PRAISE
ASKING QUESTIONS

"A must-read for any sales profe[ssional]"

—**Ben Mascarello,** Chief Operating Officer, NOVOLEX™

"Read this book. Learn the principles. Then go ask really good questions to make sure that you go win something big."

—**David Leng,** Chief Executive Officer, Sinseal Extrusions Limited

"Pay attention to this man and the lessons in this book. The system really works, and it will hugely change for the better the quality of your personal and professional relationships."

—**Timothy Armitt,** Managing Director, Lyndon Design

"My company is extremely familiar with the Sandler selling principles; we have been a client for some years. When Antonio wrote this book we made it compulsory reading. It's a very lively and engaging read that is low on technical jargon, and high on practical application. Business books are not always riveting page-turners—this one most definitely is."

—**Lyle Brambier,** President, Brambier's

ASKING QUESTIONS
THE SANDLER WAY

*Advanced Questioning Strategies
for Sales Professionals*

ANTONIO GARRIDO

© 2017 Sandler Systems, Inc. All rights reserved.

Reproduction, modification, storage in a retrieval system or retransmission, in any form or by any means, electronic, mechanical, or otherwise, is strictly prohibited without the prior written permission of Sandler Systems, Inc.

S Sandler Training (with design), Sandler, Sandler Training, Sandler Selling System, and the Sandler Pain Funnel (words and design) are registered service marks of Sandler Systems, Inc.

Sandler Submarine (words and design) is a service mark of Sandler Systems, Inc.

Because the English language lacks a generic singular pronoun that indicates both genders, we have used the masculine pronouns for the sake of style, readability, and brevity. This material applies to both men and women.

Paperback: 978-0-692-83860-0

E-book: 978-0-692-88254-2

*To my mum, Val. Maybe, just maybe,
you were right about me all along.*

*To my uniquely wonderful wife Julie, our amazing kids,
and the terrific family that supports us both.
This book would not have been possible
without the love, help, and encouragement of you all.
Thanks a million with chocky-sprinkles.*

*To those in my Sandler family,
who always seem to ask me the right questions.*

CONTENTS

ACKNOWLEDGMENTS ix

FOREWORD xi

INTRODUCTION xiii

PART 1: Run Silent, Run Deep

CHAPTER 1: The Magic of Questions 3

CHAPTER 2: Introduction to Sandler 15

CHAPTER 3: Walking though the Submarine 35

CHAPTER 4: Can We Agree to Disagree? 63

CHAPTER 5: What Are You Trying to Say? 75

PART 2: The Truth Will Set You Free

CHAPTER 6: When They Zig, You Zag 87

CHAPTER 7: You Have Your Prospect's Attention—
Now What? 97

CHAPTER 8: You Scratch My Back, I'll Scratch Yours 107

PART 3: Stop Hogging All the Airtime

CHAPTER 9: It's a Two-Way Street 121

CHAPTER 10: How to Answer Questions
   with More Questions 131

CHAPTER 11: From Knowing to Owning. 143

CHAPTER 12: Qualify, Qualify, Qualify. 153

CHAPTER 13: The Universal *Yes*. 165

CHAPTER 14: Good Questions Lead to Good Answers 179

CHAPTER 15: "How Much Time Will We Need?"
   —Questioning Master Class 189

CHAPTER 16: The Anatomy of a Sales Call. 203

EPILOGUE: Some of the Best Possible Questions to Ask 213

ACKNOWLEDGMENTS

There's not much I learned from being a bad sales professional that I couldn't have learned by simply setting all my money on fire every week. Come to think of it, that's basically what I was doing for the first phase of my sales career. My gratitude goes out to David Mattson and the entire Sandler® family for helping me stop doing that and for making the next phase of my career, and by extension this book, possible.

I am grateful, too, for the skill, tenacity, and unflagging determination of my very good friend and Sandler's resident literary genius, Yusuf Toropov, who served as developmental editor on this project. Heartfelt thanks go out to him and to his partners in crime Jerry Dorris and Laura Matthews, masters of the layout and line-editing crafts, respectively.

There are no words capable of expressing the depth of my gratitude to my brother Carlos Garrido for all the help and support he has provided over the years, so I won't pretend there are.

Deep thanks go out to all those in the Sandler home office who contributed their time, care, and attention at various phases of this project, including: Margaret Stevens Jacks, Rachel Miller, Désirée Pilachowski, Jennifer Willard, Jasamine Stephens, Elizabeth Faust, and Jena Heffernan.

Finally, thank you, dear reader, for picking up this book—and thank you in advance for continuing to read and turn the pages until you, too, stop setting all your money on fire.

FOREWORD

David Sandler, the founder of Sandler Training and the creator of the Sandler Selling System, recognized the transformative power of questions. He insisted on a professional salesperson's duty to pose good questions during the sales process—especially at those moments, early in the relationship, when buyers felt most entitled to redirect conversations with questions of their own.

Sandler rejected the "free consulting" approach to sales that doles out seemingly endless helpings of complimentary advice, insight, and experience. He challenged salespeople to spend a lot less time answering questions—and a lot more time posing them. He insisted on a salesperson's right to "reverse" a question from a prospective buyer by answering a question with a question.

This kind of selling takes practice. For most of us, it doesn't come intuitively because we've spent so much time in a sales process in which the buyer is in control and calls the shots. Now comes Antonio Garrido's book *Asking Questions the Sandler Way*. It's an invaluable, detailed, and consistently engaging elucidation of what remains, for most salespeople, a revolutionary new idea: As a professional, you have the right, and the responsibility, to take control of the sales discussion by asking good questions.

You do. If you're willing to accept that premise and take action on it, the book you're reading right now can open an exciting new chapter in your career as a professional salesperson.

David H. Mattson
President/CEO, Sandler Training

INTRODUCTION

When does the sales process really begin?

Some say that sales starts at the very first "hello." Everything before that first critical opening word, these people say, is marketing; everything after that is sales.

Others say that the real work of sales doesn't begin until the prospect first says, "No." "Otherwise," they insist, "it's just order-taking."

Those are the two most common responses; this book rejects both. This book holds that selling begins when you start asking good questions.

Most salespeople up and down the land have a fairly blunt and unsophisticated sales strategy that doesn't rely all that much on the kinds of questions you'll be reading about in this book. Their strategy is not very clever. It's not based on any clear empirical proof of success—heck, it doesn't even work that well. It is, however, familiar.

It's what typical salespeople always seem to find themselves doing. Everyone knows how unsettling it can be to try anything new or scary. The familiar sales process I'm talking about—the one most salespeople follow out of sheer force of habit—looks something like this:

- Find someone, anyone, who might be ever so slightly interested in what you do/sell/make/offer/promote.
- Beg for an appointment.
- Show up and throw up everything you know about your product or service, finding clever ways to cram as many features and benefits as you can into the time your prospect grants you.
- Agree to give your prospect everything that can possibly be asked for—if not for free, then damn close.
- Attempt a cunning closing technique or two.
- Smile as sweetly as possible.
- Keep talking fast enough, loudly enough, and engagingly enough to keep your prospect off-balance for long enough.
- Repeat the above with as many live prospects as possible.
- Chase, and chase, and chase—and hope and pray for the very best.

You know what? It actually works—but only sometimes, and not with nearly enough certainty, regularity, speed, or assuredness to keep the Pepto-Bismol at bay.

I spoke to a young, reasonably successful sales manager recently. She manages a small sales team in the IT sector at a great company. They sell an innovative, well-priced, easy-to-implement product that genuinely helps customers' raw-materials, manufacturing, and stock-management levels remain within optimal ranges, adjusting seamlessly for peaks in demand created by market variations and seasonality.

By hard work, determination, and by hook or by crook, she manages to produce the results necessary to get close enough to her monthly revenue targets on a consistent enough basis to keep her in her job.

"I never saw myself in sales," she says. (Well, who did?) "But somehow I got here. I do my very best. I read as much as I can. I work hard and try to keep my team motivated. I hope that my biggest customers will stay with me, and I hope we manage to find enough new ones along the way. But my sales targets always go up year-on-year, and my customers always want to pay less for what we give them. I have to pedal harder and harder just to stand still."

Sound familiar?

She went on, "I have a great husband and family who are OK with me spending so much time away. But it sometimes feels that I have a better relationship—and more brownie points—with the major airlines than I do with my kids. I feel like I should be much further ahead in my career than I am."

Since she decided to get into sales and sales management, however (she told me), she sleeps like a baby.

"Really?" I asked.

"Yes," she answered, without missing a beat. "Sometimes I wake up in the middle of the night screaming at the top of my lungs."

"Oh dear," I said.

"Things will get better, though," she insisted. "Never lose hope. Positive attitude and all that."

I had to break the news to her. In today's modern, increasingly sophisticated and demanding world, "hope" is not really much of a high-growth strategy.

Students of the Sandler Selling System® methodology quickly learn that selling is not about lists of compelling features and benefits; it's not about clever closes or flashy literature and expensive marketing collateral. It's not about hogging all the airtime in the meeting, nor is it about forcing your own agenda into the buying process. It's not about jazzy presentations or brow-beating the other guy into submission.

What is it about, then? It's all about reaching non-threatening, incremental agreements to proceed. It's about asking, not telling. It's about listening, not talking. It's about asking just the right question, in just the right way, for just the right reason, at just the right time to help prospects discover for themselves whether you and your product or service are just right for them.

The most successful salespeople the world over have discovered the secret of sales success: asking exactly the right questions, and then shutting up and letting prospects discover for themselves that you're exactly the right fit for their needs. It is letting prospects discover that they have compelling needs, and genuine reasons to buy. The most successful salespeople know that:

- The best way to discover the truth (the real truth, mind you—not the stuff prospects want you to believe because they think it's in their best interests to keep you guessing) is to ask really smart questions.
- The best way, the only way, to understand what clients really need is to understand their situation—by asking the right questions.
- The best way to demonstrate knowledge is to ask the right questions.
- The best way to keep prospects on the right path is to ask the right questions.
- The best way to reduce waste, increase efficiency and effectiveness, and identify exactly the right solution for everybody's needs is (you guessed it) to ask the right questions.

Introduction

This is why this book will come in handy.

Perhaps you're wondering: Why don't salespeople do this naturally? Why don't salespeople instinctively ask the right sorts of questions, at the right times, in such a way as to encourage the prospect to do the right thing—namely, tell the whole truth—and honestly assess whether it makes sense to buy or invest in the particular products, services, or partnerships?

There is indeed a worldwide buyer-seller disconnect. The reason it exists is that salespeople don't naturally ask the right questions. The main reason for this is that people are programmed and conditioned from childhood not to ask too many questions. Quite the contrary: People are programmed to answer questions.

At school, children are rewarded for giving good (i.e., accurate, school-board approved) answers. They usually aren't rewarded for asking good, probing questions that explore the assumptions of others. In fact, a lot of us were reprimanded for doing just that!

Most of us are all too familiar with the "why game" that young children adopt at around two or three or four years old. It sounds something like this: "Why is the sky blue? Why do we get old? Why do I have to eat spinach?" And so on. Eventually, some exhausted grownup gives a variation on this answer: "Look, I don't know—just because! Stop asking so many questions. Go to your room and play." Eventually, we learn to stop asking.

On top of this, people are culturally encouraged to get along, to ingratiate, to integrate, to blend in. No one wants to appear different; people are pressured to conform, to avoid rocking the boat. If you don't believe this, think about what happens to kids in kindergarten or first grade who don't do what they're expected to do in class. Yes, it's a short visit to the naughty-corner—again.

What's more, it's stamped on human DNA not to take risks, not to stick our heads out of the entrance to the cave, or above the parapet. There is an evolutionary component to this: The animal that strays too far from the safety of the pack gets singled out, leapt upon, and devoured in a particularly nasty, colorful, and sharp-toothed way. Individuals with genes that say, "Go on, give it a try, what's the worst that can happen?," somehow found themselves on the dinner menu and not able, obviously, to pass on their risk-taking genes to the next generation. Sometimes survival of the fittest is simply a matter of doing what everyone else is doing.

But—and this is key—"doing what everyone else is doing" is not the recipe for survival among successful salespeople.

IN SEARCH OF THE RIGHT QUESTIONS

This book is about asking the right questions so that both the seller and the buyer discover the right solution as efficiently and as effectively as possible—even if they discover that the right solution right now is for the prospect to buy from the competition. "What?" I hear you cry. "Sacrilege! This can't be!" Sorry—it's sad, but true.

This book is about not looking, sounding, or thinking like the average salesperson. It's about keeping barriers down and communication lines open. It's about getting to the right solution, faster, more efficiently, more smoothly, and less painfully. It's about asking the right questions, in the right way, at the right time, for the right reason. It's about asking questions the Sandler way.

Whether you're making millions or you find that there's just too much week left at the end of your paycheck, this book is for you. My aim is to teach you the theory, the practical skills, the confidence, and the specific applications necessary to know exactly what to ask, along with when, how, and why. My aim is to make you much more successful than you have ever been.

The key to successful questioning skills, you will find, lies not in simply preparing a list of a few hundred clever questions, learning them by rote, and trotting out the exact right question at just the right time. No, the key lies in getting your mind right, your beliefs right, your attitudes right, your habits right, and your understanding right—and this book will help with these things. Questioning skill, you will realize, lies in changing your habits, modifying your beliefs, and resisting your biological and sociological programming—a daunting, yet immensely rewarding journey.

So my first official question to you, dear reader, is: Shall we begin? Good. Turn the page.

> *"Judge a man by his questions rather than his answers."*
> —Voltaire

PART 1

Run Silent, Run Deep

What is the Buyer-Seller Dance?
What is the Sandler Submarine?
What is the most successful questioning model for salespeople?

CHAPTER 1

The Magic of Questions

Picture this scene:

A magician is framed in the spotlight.

Standing stock still, he holds his right hand high in the air.

In a display of incredible prowess and skill borne of countless hours of diligent practice, he shuffles a pack of cards with a single gloved hand.

His fingers are almost invisible with the speed and dexterity of the routine.

Every eye in the house is opened wide and locked on the pack bathed in the spotlight.

Every mouth hangs open in amazement and wonder.

Oooooh!

However, his left hand, the one tucked just behind his lapel, is where the real action is taking place. That's where your card is, by the way—not in the pack high in the air that transfixes everyone else.

Magicians rely on audiences falling prey to that kind of misdirection—and that's OK. That's what the show is all about, after all. It's the "I'm cleverer than you" hour. For the purposes of entertainment, audiences allow themselves to be fooled. Or, perhaps for the purposes of discovery, audiences will try to figure out what's going on. How did he swallow the card, or catch the knife, or predict the name of that young lady's grandmother? Either way, audiences accept it all with good grace; that's the complicit part of the performance.

However, when prospects and clients play the "I'm cleverer than you game" with salespeople, or worse, when salespeople try to play the "I'm cleverer than you" game with prospects, unintentionally or otherwise, very unhelpful things begin to unfold.

Prospects, like magicians on the stage, will often intentionally withhold important information. They will misdirect. They will ask smokescreen questions and provide you with evasive answers or half-truths intended to keep you off balance and keep your eyes and attention looking in entirely the wrong direction.

WHAT'S REALLY GOING ON?

Salespeople need to first recognize that not every word, every statement, every nuance, or every suggestion that prospects make is intended to help them fully understand the situation. Just like the magician on stage, some of what you see and hear in a sales call is deliberately intended to misdirect. Salespeople need to try to decode what is being said (or not said); they need to try to peer behind the curtain, through the dry-ice smoke, and behind the mirror. They need to decipher what's really going on and not let themselves become distracted by the gloved hand in the spotlight. They need to keep the conversation focused and on topic.

When prospects ask you a question (or use wishy-washy words, try to mislead you, or use smokescreen tactics), wouldn't it be nice if you knew for sure what the true intention behind it was? David Sandler developed a tool to help the salesperson accomplish exactly this. It's called reversing.

For now, all I want you to notice is that, often, prospects will make statements which, when you dig a little below the surface, can be interpreted in a number of different ways.

For instance: When a prospect says, "We've been working with XYZ Company since my parents started the business nearly 50 years ago," does that statement mean:

- "I'm looking for a brand new solution"?
- "I'm never going to change such a longstanding family tradition"?
- "I'm glad you came along; I didn't know there were any alternatives"?

Well, you have two options when it comes to deciphering what's behind the prospect's statement. Either:

- Take yourself hence to a cave perilously high in the misty mountains. Clothe yourself only in rags, and, sleeping on hay, fast for 40 days and nights. Mediate 18 hours a day to properly attune yourself into the psychic ether, and divine what the prospect might have meant by slaughtering a chicken and watching how the smoke from its charred feathers swirls in the moonlight at the stroke of midnight, on the eve of the summer solstice...

Or:

- Ask.

I have always plumped for the second option; I'm not good with heights, and sleeping on hay gives me a nasty rash.

Interpreting a statement as a question and then attempting to answer it (even though you don't know what was behind it all) is a mistake—often a fatal one. "Never answer an unasked question"— that's Sandler Rule #5 of 49 if you're keeping score at home.*

Before responding appropriately to prospects' statements (and remember, sometimes the best response is merely a nod, a smile, or a shrug; sometimes the statement made is merely a statement, and doesn't require a response), you must first discover the intent of the statement.

You do this by asking:

- "You are telling me that because…?"
- "OK, but that means what?"
- "And…?"
- "Such as…?"

Those are reverses, by the way. You're going to be learning a lot about reverses later on in the book.

Let's see how this approach could help you deal with the example from above.

> "We've been working with XYZ Company since my parents started the business 50 years ago."
>
> "OK, I understand. You're telling me that because…?"
>
> "Well, I'm running things now, and I think it's maybe time for a change—we have to move with the times, after all."

Nice. Not a single decapitated chicken nor trip to the chemist for some ointment for that bothersome rash. But keep going, it's not quite over yet.

---

* See *The Sandler Rules: 49 Timeless Selling Principles and How to Apply Them*

"Makes sense. But tell me, what does 'move with the times' mean in your view?"

By adopting this simple yet powerful technique to explore what the prospect is truly saying, feeling, or meaning, the salesperson ensures that real roadblocks are uncovered. At the same time, the salesperson is not jumping to any erroneous conclusions. All too often, salespeople make mountains out of molehills. This is because they don't bother to figure out the underlying meaning of utterances that were, after all, just statements.

DOES THE PROSPECT DESERVE YOUR TIME AND ATTENTION?

Most novice and rookie salespeople tend to treat every prospect in their funnel with equal importance. Or, if they do try to decide that some deserve more attention than others, they tend to choose the most lucrative opportunities to invest most of their time and effort and energy.

I suppose that seems natural and obvious. However, the truth is that the more effort you put into qualifying an opportunity, the more quickly you can develop and close it (or elect to discount it, of course). Often salespeople spend way too much time pursuing particular opportunities merely based on a hunch, rather than having objectively identified and prioritized its value. The "first-in, first-out" method is hugely inefficient; so, too, is the "biggest first"—especially when neither of these methods are measured against the correct qualification criteria that you set.

NOTE: You, not the prospect.

According to Sandler, your qualification criteria should be stringent, and should include three key gates:

- Pain: What does the gap look like between where the prospects are and where they want to be?
- Budget: Are the prospects willing and able to commit time, resources, energy, money, people, etc., to have that gap closed?
- Decision: Do you know who from both sides needs to be involved in the decision-making process—where they are, when the decision will be made, and why it has to be that way?

Time and again salespeople invest the time, the money, the effort, and the distraction of putting together a whizz-bang presentation to deliver to people who, in the final analysis, should not have even been on the salesperson's radar. Why not? They were not genuine prospects—the salespeople did not properly qualify the opportunity against these three key criteria. Without having a detailed understanding of these three elements, it is impossible to predict which opportunities you should be working on first, which you are the best fit for, or which have the greatest possibility of success.

So ask.

What's the alternative? Guessing?

No, seriously. Ask.

PAIN—WHERE'S THE GAP?

People buy for a variety of reasons, of course. But, their most basic purchase motivation is to bridge the gap between where they are and where they want to be. David Sandler described this gap as "pain."

Pain is the first and the most important step in the qualification process, and it is the first Go/No-Go gate to determine whether prospects qualify to receive any further attention from you. To be clear, if the prospect does not have a compelling, measurable, and quantifiable issue that you can solve, what's the point in pursuing things further?

People sometimes say that great salespeople are so good that they can sell ice in a snowstorm. The reason that that analogy even makes sense is because what a person in a snowstorm typically doesn't need more of is ice. However, it stands to reason that the bigger, more present, and more compelling a prospect's pain is, the more motivated the prospect will be to alleviate it. When prospects describe their pains by using emotionally charged language, typically their motivation to fix things is much more heightened. The best salespeople will key into that and make it work to the sale's advantage.

FUDWACA

FUDWACA is an acronym for a quick overview of the kinds of things you'll hear when prospects are in pain:

- "We're **frustrated** by the results around..."
- "I'm so **upset** that this hasn't gotten any better..."
- "The last guy so **disappointed** us, he..."
- "We are so **worried** about..."
- "The board members are **anxious** that this gets fixed..."
- "We're **concerned** that..."
- "Whenever that happens, I get so **angry** because..."

You get the idea.

OK, so a prospect is upset. So what? It's a puzzle that needs figuring out.

Imagine you're on the side of the busy road. It's rush hour. It's raining. It's dark. You've got a flat tire. You're late to pick up the kids. Your trunk is full of junk. You've got no tools to change the tire, and you don't have a spare anyway. You're wearing your most expensive work clothes, including leather dress shoes. Nightmare.

Imagine that a magic genie appears demanding payment for one wish.

He can fix the tire with the mere wave of a hand—right now. Instantly. Within 20 seconds, you'll be on your way to get the kids.

What would you give the genie in exchange for the immediate favor?

A lot, I'm guessing. Why? Because you're in real, immediate, and compelling pain.

Consider this possibility. Your prospect, the new production manager of a small engineering firm, describes that her production output is behind target because every few weeks two critical machines in the plant keep breaking down.

You sell preventative maintenance of just such machinery. A great prospect? Well maybe, maybe not. Let's dig a little deeper.

Instead of telling her what your company does best, you should first ask what each separate breakdown costs her in time, effort, energy, people, resources, dollars, etc.

Then you ask what the knock-on or other indirect costs are—lost labor, overtime, unhappy customers, damaged brand, etc.

Then you ask if all of that is a little, or a lot.

Then you ask specifically how the company's most important customers have responded to the delays in shipping.

Then you ask how long this has been happening.

Then you ask what she and her team have done to fix it.

Then you ask what it might mean in her world if the genie (you) appeared and magically fixed it all.

Then you ask if she's given up trying to address the issue.

All of these questions help you to understand what Sandler

calls the "pain puzzle"—three elements of pain that can help you determine what your prospect's peace of mind is worth.

1. The Observed Problem: What's going on?
2. The Causes of the Problem: Why is this going on?
3. The Impact of the Problem: How does this reveal itself in the prospect's world?

WHAT PAINS DO YOU ADDRESS?

Write down the answers to these questions:

- Specifically, what does your product or service do for your clients?
- What problems/issues does it enable them to solve or avoid?
- What desirable results does it facilitate?
- What does having your particular brand of magic-sauce enable them to do better?
- What efficiencies can they take advantage of by having your products and services at their disposal?

Once you have a clear understanding of why your prospects might be interested in the things that you fix—the pain gaps that you close—you should be able to list a number of pain indicators (issues that your prospects typically describe to you) that you can potentially address.

If, in conversation with your prospects and the application of good questioning skills, you are able to uncover that your prospect: a) has some of these pain indicators, b) is aware that there is an issue or issues, and c) is aware that you are a potential source of a better future, then it's time to decide whether or not you should continue the process to discuss the investment of time, money, attention, and political capital that will be required to close the gap. If not, you need to close the file.

I'm talking about asking something like this:

"Alex, imagine what your world might look like if you didn't have to keep dealing with this issue. You know, we have been rather successful working with other companies just like yours to accomplish significant manufacturing output increases, shorter lead times, and reduced costs. It sounds to me like it might be somewhat valuable to take a closer look in determining whether or not we could work with you in the same way. I don't suppose it might make sense to invest, say, an hour or so to meet for you to show me the bottlenecks and issues, and for us to figure out whether what we have done for others might work for you, too? Would you be comfortable with that—does that sound fair?"

If you hear crickets, it's maybe time to move on. You can't help everyone, and you certainly can't help people who don't want help.

IS YOUR PROSPECT WILLING AND ABLE?

If you have uncovered your prospects' pain and properly understood the pain puzzle as it applies to their world specifically, it's time to figure out what they are prepared to invest to make their world a better place (reduce the pain gap).

You need prospects and clients who are both willing and able to invest in your solutions. At Sandler we believe that willingness to invest is even more important than ability since if willingness is high enough, prospects will work harder to find the budget to solve their problem—their pain. Remember: No pain, no sale.

This is not always just a simple money issue. Often prospects have the budget, but not the staff, time, patience, wherewithal, skills, motivation, or mental bandwidth to even implement your solution. In which case, no sale. Just wanting it is not enough. They have to be able to invest in it, invest in the implementation, and invest in the use of it. If just wanting it were enough, I'd have that brand new Ferrari out in my driveway right now.

Let me go take a look out the window to check.

Nope.

There's a parallel rule: No money, no sale. Later in the book we will review the kinds of questions to ask to uncover the magnitude of investment that prospects may be willing to provide in order to close their pain gap.

Finally, there's a third rule to consider: No clear decision process, no sale. Whose decision is it, anyway? How will it be made? By whom? When? This is the final element for qualifying/disqualifying a potential sales opportunity.

Remember: If the prospect isn't qualified, you don't make a presentation. Period.

Later in the book, we will explore the kinds of issues that you need to uncover and understand before electing to invest your time, money, effort, energy in presenting, or even quoting the project in the first place.

CHAPTER SUMMARY

- Prioritize your prospects by using the pain, budget, and decision process.
- By asking better questions, learn to uncover what the prospect is really saying/asking, and why.

> *The real magic is in truth and honesty and openness.*
> *—Frank Ocean*

CHAPTER 2

Introduction to Sandler

David H. Sandler, the creator of the Sandler Selling System, had an inquisitive nature. He was curious about what made success possible. He realized that real success (in any arena, not just sales) lay in understanding and mastering three critical areas: behaviors, attitudes, and techniques.

He realized that with the right **behavior** (doing the right amount of the right kinds of things), coupled with the right **technique** (doing things correctly, with skill, understanding, and dexterity), all with the right **attitude** (the voice between your ears that says, "Yes, you're worthy," or, "Yes, you can do it," or, "Just one more push") can help achieve what at first seems impossible. It can move mountains; ants and rubber-tree plants; rams and dams, and all that.

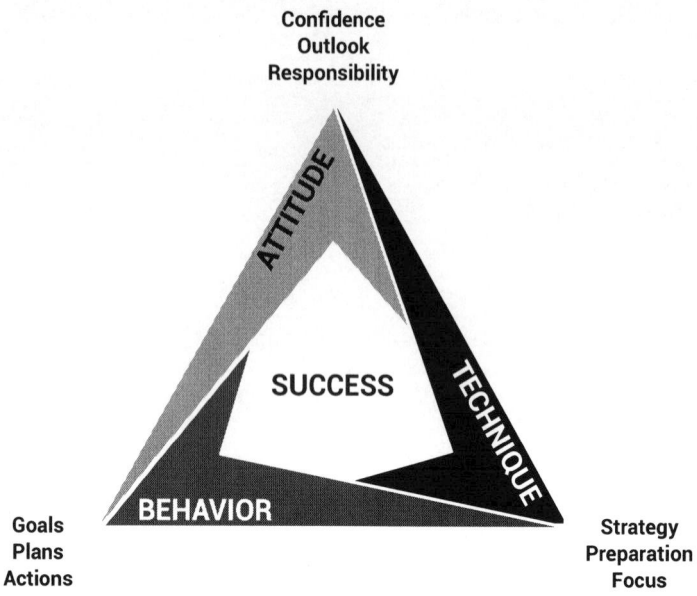

Sandler went on to discover that it isn't how you feel that determines how you act; rather, it's how you act that determines how you feel. Think about going to the gym. You know how creative you can be when trying to think of reasonable excuses not to go? It's too cold, it's too late (or too early), your legs hurt, you've got a headache, your sock drawer desperately needs rearranging, etc. But then think about how energized, virtuous, and thoroughly fabulous you feel after you've gone.

Sandler discovered that the quickest way to self-confidence is to do something that you're scared of or that you don't want to do. Not only that, but the internal scripting that you give yourself and the way that you see yourself—your conception of yourself, your company, your market, and so on—all of that is critical to your performance, your skill, your staying power, your determination, your drive and ambition, and, ultimately, your success.

Remember this rule*:

SUCCESS = FAILURE + PERSISTENCE

Another key element of human behavior deeply embedded in the Sandler theory is something called transactional analysis. (No, it's not an advanced accounting course, but good guess.) Transactional analysis, known as TA to its closest friends, was developed in the 1950s by psychiatrist Eric Berne. TA is based on the fact that humans are social creatures who interact with others in very predictable and easily understood (and therefore easy to manage) ways. TA practitioners believe that the best approach to understanding the human condition is a robust theory for personal growth and change based on three primary ego states: Parent, Adult, and Child.

Think of these three characters (ego states) as separate voices in your head. It might sound icky (or at least a little overcrowded), but everyone's got these three ego states at play. Berne, and later Sandler, realized that the three modalities of behavior manifest themselves in specific ways that have applications to the selling and commercial environment.

These manifestations are based around achieving a level of OK-ness. This is a theory of human communication that can be extended to the analysis and understanding of not only people, but social structures and organizations, too. Organizations, after all, are built from a group of individuals.

WHAT DO YOU MEAN, OK-NESS?

Defining the terms is a common question at this point of the discussion. In any interaction with another individual, there are, at

---

* "You have to learn to fail, to win." Sandler Rule #1

any given point in time, four possible OK-ness states at play. Take a look:

I'm OK, and you're OK.

A healthy position. You feel good about yourself and your capabilities and competencies; others, in turn, feel the same way.

(Lovely. Let's share a cookie.)

I'm OK, and you're not OK.

You feel good about yourself in this position, but you see others as damaged, incapable, or unhappy.

(Not lovely. I have cookies—you have no cookies.)

I'm not OK, and you're OK.

The salesperson's plight.

You may have heard of the Golden Rule as adapted to the world of sales: He who has the gold makes all the rules. That's this position.

In this position, salespeople see themselves as the weaker partners in the buyer-seller relationship and buyers are better. Salespeople who hold this position will subconsciously accept abuse or poor treatment—and resign themselves to it.

(Not lovely. You have all the cookies—I have no cookies. I really like cookies.)

I'm not OK, and you're not OK.

A bad situation, all around.

This is the worst position in which to be. It means that you believe that you are in a terrible state and the rest of the world is just as bad. Consequently there is no hope for help and support.

You think, "I am doomed. We are all doomed."

(Deeply unlovely. No one has cookies!)

TA goes further. It explains how people's behaviors and beliefs as adults have been formed as young children in particular and far-reaching ways. According to TA, people develop their meaning, understanding, and life scripts at an early age (before the ages of 6 or 7). These scripts continue to play in people's heads in their mature and adult lives. This "scripting" determines how they see and value themselves as adults, how they interact with others, and how they set self-limiting beliefs—or, even worse, allow others to do so on their behalf.

WHAT'S ALL THIS ABOUT VOICES?

At first glance, this might all sound rather deterministic and fatalistic, with everyone falling prey to the vagaries of dismembered and commanding head voices. If what I've shared thus far feels like a case of, "You keep him talking, I'll get the net," please hear me out.

The good news is that people can elect to decide or teach themselves their own new roles and scripts in the drama of their own lives. They can decide their own destiny—change the script, change the story, and change the ending. All destructive decisions can be changed, and all emotional difficulties are entirely curable. Hoorah! Cookies for everyone, after all.

Proponents of TA aim to move toward adult autonomy (freedom from damaging or limiting childhood scripting), spontaneity, intimacy, and problem solving, as opposed to avoidance or passivity.

There are three dominant scripts—those ego states (i.e., voices)—that adults carry around with them every second of their lives. Yes, I said every single second—awake or asleep. Slightly unsettling and creepy, I know, but there you go. They are the Parent, the Adult, and the Child.

P — **Parent Ego State**
Behavior, thoughts, and feelings copied from parents or parental figures

A — **Adult Ego State**
Behaviors and thoughts as direct responses to the here and now

C — **Child Ego State**
Behaviors, thoughts, and feelings replayed from childhood

The Parent ego state

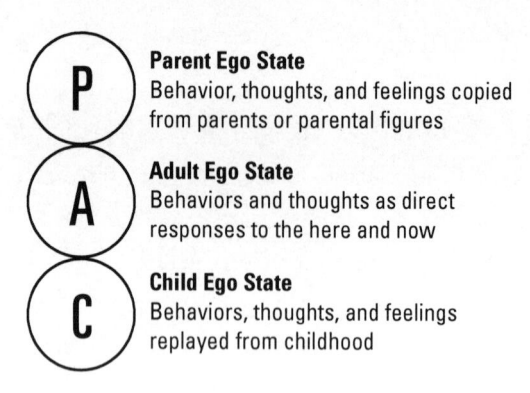

The Parent ego state is where the information about good/bad, right/wrong, appropriate/inappropriate is stored.

The Adult ego state

Here houses the logical, analytical, rational part of the brain that weighs pros and cons, pluses and minuses, upsides and downsides. It's the engineer.

The Child ego state

Here you have the realm of emotions and feelings, wants and desires.

The Child is especially easy to recognize. It's the little six-year-old child inside us all who demands the ice cream and is in the grip of a class-A, DEFCON-6 hissy-meltdown fit when a squirrel suddenly appears and all thoughts of ice cream are forgotten in an instant.

It's the voice that says, "I want this," or "I want that"; it also says, "I don't want this," or "I don't want that."

Here is the genius of the story: Sandler realized that while sellers have all of this scripting constantly at play, buyers do, too.

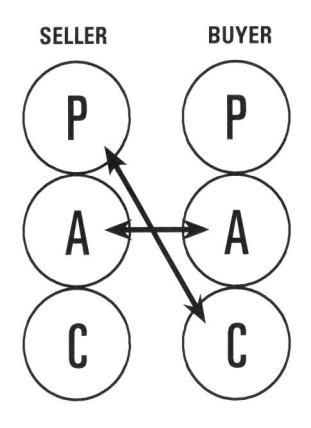

We do not want an Adult-to-Adult conversation. The seller, using Nurturing Parent tonality, engages the buyer's Child ego state.

This leads buyers to behave in certain predictable TA ways. Sandler connected the dots. "People make buying decisions emotionally…and then justify those decisions intellectually," he famously said.

So if a seller can help a prospect's Child discover that he wants something, the prospect's Adult will consider it and justify the plan to the prospect's Parent, who will then jointly decide whether to allow it. But remember: If the Child doesn't actually start the conversation, nothing happens at all. It all starts with the Child ego state wanting something.

Therefore, to properly kick-start the buying process, the seller has to first engage the Child's emotional response, establish a desire to buy, and then make sure that when the other voices in the buyer's head demand their airtime on the matter, they get what they want, too. Otherwise, nothing moves forward.

HOW THE PARENT/ADULT/CHILD DYNAMIC WORKS IN REAL LIFE

Picture this: A fully-grown, rational, well-balanced, well-tailored businessperson walks past a certain well-known "fruity" computer store and sees a brand new light-as-a-feather shiny laptop on display with crowds of eager new shoppers milling round the newly launched gleaming machine—all billing and cooing and salivating wildly.

Child: Ooh, I want a new laptop! That one, there.

Adult: Why? What's wrong with the one you have?

Child: Don't like it.

Adult: Why not? Anyway, can we really afford a new one right now?

Child: Don't care. I want that one—the old one isn't as good as that one.

Parent: Are you sure you're not acting too impulsively? Have you thought about this?

Adult: Let's check out specifications, prices, and benefits of the latest ranges, and then decide. Is that fair?

Child: No. I want that one.

Parent: Look, if it makes sense, and it will help us to get our work done better and faster, and we'll have the latest security and operating system, then maybe it seems like it might be a good idea. [Notice that the Parent is the one who uses words like "good" and "bad," not the Adult.]

Adult: Well, OK, that makes sense.

Child: Yay! Quick, that one!

Based on this exchange, who do you think the fruity-computer people want to engage first? The Child! Then the Parent and the Adult. The clever marketers at the fruity computer's company have gone to great lengths and extraordinary expense to air commercials at appropriate times on appropriate channels showing...

- …the Child (in flashing and fast-moving blocks of bright primary colors and interesting swooshing sounds) how exciting the new laptop would be to own.
- …the Parent how reasonable the whole thing is when compared to the cost of the same machines only a year ago.
- …the Adult how sensible it would be to have the latest antivirus software and how light, portable, multimodal, and adaptable the new design is.

Clever buggers.

LOOK WHO'S TALKING

At the heart of all David Sandler's discoveries was one single word: understanding.

When you seek to understand, you seek to move closer—to break down barriers, to facilitate harmony and accord. You gain understanding by learning, and you learn by questioning. In today's modern selling and commercial environment, this is a universally accepted (if often ignored) tenet. But at the time that Sandler discovered and developed these theories, he broke new ground and formed the basis for a sales, sales management, and leadership training enterprise with a global footprint that has the power to change the outcomes of countless sales exchanges in countless ways.

Recognizing that all of the prospect's voices come into play at various points during the sales process, Sandler set about developing a systemized sales and prospecting methodology that ensured every aspect of the interaction remains balanced, fair, and equitable with minimal discord or frustration. He realized that from the buyer's perspective, the Child needed to be genuinely interested and engaged; only then could the Adult and Parent concerns be addressed as well. The latter two would determine how and under what conditions the process would be allowed to continue (or not).

NOTE: For more information on transactional analysis and how it applies to the modern selling environment, contact your local Sandler Sales and Management coach. Details can be found at www.sandler.com/training-centers.

YOU AREN'T WHAT YOU DO

Sandler, with a new understanding of the tenets of TA, found a way to not only systemize the elements of the sales process, but also to help beleaguered and feckless salespeople remain mentally healthy and resilient. He did this by teaching salespeople how to separate the identity self from the sales role self. This is the heart of the Sandler Selling System: the Identity/Role (I/R) Theory of sales.

I/R Theory boils down to this: You are not what you do for a living. Your identity is who you are on the inside, not what you do for a paycheck.

Take a minute to roll that one around in your mind a few times. You probably won't come across a bigger or more important idea all day.

When people are asked as children what they want to be when they grow up, they usually say, "Doctor," or "Senator," or "Soccer player," or some such.* They never seem to say, "I want to be happy," or "I want to be tall." People describe what their future self will look like based on what they are interested in and what they hope they will be getting paid to do. What's more, people seem to ascribe (or have it ascribed to them by the cultural norms) certain values, beliefs, and expectations of happiness based on some level of success in their future role and its earning potential.

---

* If there are kids out there genuinely hoping to become lifelong servers at national fast-food restaurant chains, I haven't run into any of them yet.

The rule seems to be:

LOTS OF MONEY = A GOOD THING
LITTLE MONEY = A BAD THING

Society encourages and highly prizes aspirations toward lawyer or entrepreneur over artist or poet, based on how society views, rewards, and values these vocations and professions.

Things get more complicated when parents admonish and chide their children for performing badly in a task or making a significant enough mistake to attract adult attention. Then parents may say things like, "You're such a bad boy for having broken the window pane," or, "What a bad girl for making your brother cry like that." In other words, how the child performs in a task is rewarded or punished on a personal level. Instead, the parents should say, "That was a bad thing you just did," and not, "What a bad person you are for having done that thing."

The result? As children, people are programmed to confuse the person with the performance. Good performance = good person; bad performance = bad person.

As people grow up, therefore, they are programmed to blur the boundaries between what they do (actions and roles) and who they are (values and beliefs).

As an adult, you might have a wide variety of roles: husband, wife, sister, teacher, committee member, etc. But these things are not, Sandler realized, who you are. Who you are is private, hidden, that voice in your head; that's your true identity. What you do, what the world sees—that is your role.

"Who you 'I' (identity) is not what you 'R' (role)," said Sandler. He went on to discover that if you see yourself poorly (your identity—your self-image, self-confidence, self-talk, self-belief, etc., as scoring pretty low on the ability/capability/

worthiness scale), then you will never achieve as much in your role performance.

If you believe that you're a loser when it comes to life in general, guess what? You'll be a loser in your chosen role, too. Conversely, if you firmly believe, think, and know that you're a good person and a true winner with good values, good commandments, good ethos, good beliefs, etc., you will go on to perform better at being a spouse, professional, parent, and so on.

What does that mean, in practical terms? It means if you have a bad sales day at the office, it's just that—a bad sales day. It doesn't mean that you're a bad salesperson. Keep your "I" and your "R" separate, dear reader. Be careful how you bring up your children and the messaging you give them, too—keep their bad performances separate from your bad messaging.

To further understand the complicated interaction between the salesperson and the buyer, David Sandler examined the interplay—the dynamics—between the two. He wanted to know what a typical sales process looked like and who was in charge, meaning who was subservient to whom, when, and, perhaps most importantly, why.

Sandler also wanted to know what could be done to alter that dynamic in such a way as to increase understanding, respect, and equanimity between the parties. Sandler trainers call this dynamic the Buyer-Seller Dance.

SHALL WE DANCE?

Typically, in the Buyer-Seller Dance, buyers are in charge of the interaction between their companies and that of the salesperson. The seller dances to the buyer's tune. The buyers get all the salesperson's goodies. The salesperson gets the runaround. The buyers get what they want; the seller gets shafted. Nice—not!

It looks like this when the buyer leads the dance (which is, let's face it, most of the time):

	SELLER		BUYERS
STEP 1	↓	Prospect	Play cards close to the vest
STEP 2	↓	Present	Demand and receive unpaid consultancy
STEP 3	↓	Attempt Close	Avoid commitment
STEP 4	↓	Chase	Disappear

Let's look at this in a little more detail, shall we?

STEP 1

From the seller's perspective

You, the seller, do some prospecting to find a likely candidate for your goods or services. This prospecting activity can take many forms, cost many dollars, and take a very long time—but, for the sake of brevity here, let's just say that by fair means or foul, a potential buyer seems to show some glimmer of interest in you and your shiny wares.

You immediately express your undying gratitude at being so favored and begin to do all you can to ingratiate yourself in the eyes of the prospect. Nothing could possibly be too much trouble at all, ever. "Don't be silly," you say. "Of course I can get the proposal to you by Monday morning. I'm sure I will have other children getting married before too long; I'm sure I can watch the video of the ceremony after I have done this proposal for you."

The main thing, you believe, is that you have found someone new to pitch. Lovely!

From the buyer's perspective

The idea on this side is pretty simple. The buyer takes pains to ensure that the truth, the whole truth, and nothing but the truth never sees the light of day. He will mislead you, the seller, regarding: his real level of interest; who else he may be talking to; his past experiences; his real motivation; his real budget; the real extent of his purchasing guidelines; what he is used to paying; why he is talking to you right now, and so on.

He will do all that he can to remain in a position of authority. He will obfuscate, mislead, and misrepresent.

Remember, he believes that it's perfectly OK to mislead a salesperson. He believes you can indulge in that sort of behavior and still get to heaven—and he practices doing so almost every day.

STEP 2

From the seller's perspective

Being the trusting (and sometimes, desperate) soul that you are, you believe (or choose to believe) all or nearly all of the buyer's hogwash. Based on that belief, you swing into action, which sometimes includes involving other people, departments, or functions. You now have a new purpose in life—that of dealing with the prospect's RFI, RFP, and RFQ (and sometimes, BS) and of presenting to him all of the compelling reasons that you are simply the 100% best, most obvious supplier to use.

If the buyer is lucky, you may even treat him to one of your killer slide presentations. You are really good at slide presentations, after all; you went to that really expensive course once.

It's features and benefits time, folks.

Razzle-dazzle 'em!

From the buyer's perspective

The buyer thinks: "Another highly paid, highly experienced, highly motivated (and rather gullible) young soul is going to teach me all about his world: all about the strengths and weaknesses of his competitors; how the market is moving; his 'secret sauce'; and, best of all, he's going to do it at my place, to my timetable, under my terms and conditions, answering all of my questions—and for free. Goody."

STEP 3

From the seller's perspective

Presentation over.

Quotation sent.

Brochures delivered.

Slide presentation handed over on a brightly colored, company branded memory stick, which the marketing department took six weeks to select.

Now the real "sales" work begins—finally! You get to do what you are paid to do: close the deal.

Time to break out the sales training book that you were given your first day on the job. It's "trial close" time. Lights. Camera. Action!

Some salespeople prefer the "alternate close": "Would you like the A model or the B model?" Really? In this day and age, the alternate close? Really? Oh, the cunning, the guile. The prospect will never see that one coming, you sly old silver-tongued fox!

Others take this opportunity to whip out the "Ben Franklin

close"—it's pros and cons time. All the reasons the prospect shouldn't buy go on one side; all the reasons he should buy go on the other side. I wonder which list will come out longer. Don't forget to draw the diagram, of course; it really helps when you draw the diagram. Puuuulease!

Let's not leave out the old "assumptive close." "When we deliver, what address should we use?" What about the "challenge close," or the "major/minor close," or my old favorite, the "back up the hearse and let them smell the flowers close."

There are a million different closes. Guess what? Once you take away the law of averages, they simply don't work. Because buyers have seen and heard them all.

From the buyer's perspective

Closing time is coming. Get ready. Phasers on stun. Repel all intruders.

The prospect will smile sweetly and sound completely sincere as he thanks you for your efforts. He reminds you that his board meets next Tuesday, and he couldn't possibly pass the order until the managing director signs it off personally. Ask him to call you Wednesday morning—that'll do the trick.

STEP 4

From the seller's perspective

Hmm. You called Wednesday morning just as agreed—he was in a meeting. You think, *Probably some emergency.*

You left a message. *He's sure to call back soon.*

You wait a few days, and then send a light and breezy email. *I don't want to pressure him. I hope he's OK. Should I send flowers?*

You text. *I hope that's not being too pushy.*

Another email. Another weekend. Voicemail jail.
I'll wait a while...and a while...and a while more. I might pop round with donuts next week—"I was just passing by."
After six weeks of radio-silence, you might get the hint.

From the buyer's perspective

He is hiding from you. He is firmly ensconced in the Buyer Witness Protection Program. He has changed his name and address and has had his facial structure rearranged by a nice young surgeon with very white teeth. "If the salesperson from ABC Company calls, tell him I suddenly left the company and I moved to Guatemala."

WHY, WHY, WHY?

Let's be honest with each other—and with ourselves. The above is what usually happens.

"But why," I hear you cry, "do we put up with all of this nonsense and abuse?"

Well, dear reader, you put up with it for two main reasons:

1. It works. It's brutal, it's ugly, it's hugely inefficient, it puts the buyer firmly in the driving seat, it beats the crap out of you (the seller), prices tumble, you waste almost all of your productive selling time—but it works. You make some sales. Sometimes. (Actually, it's the law of averages that is working, on that rare occasion, not the dance steps, but let's leave that aside for now.)
2. You don't know, or have confidence in, any other way.

Fortunately, this book will give you a better way. Strap yourself in; it's going to be a white-knuckle ride.

What's a better selling system? The Sandler Selling System, that's what.

Take a look at this brief outline to see if, even on some intuitive level, it feels slightly more equitable and thorough than the old, inefficient Buyer-Seller Dance where you're following, not leading.

DISCOVERY PHASE

Step 1: Bonding & Rapport

- Interrupt the pattern that the buyer expects.

Step 2: Up-Front Contract

- Agree to what is on everyone's agenda, up front.

QUALIFICATION PHASE

Step 3: Pain

- Explore and understand the compelling reason(s) to buy.

Step 4: Budget

- Determine what's needed in terms of time, money, effort, and energy.

Step 5: Decision

- Identify the full cast of decision makers, and what they each want to see happen.

PRESENTATION PHASE

Step 6: Fulfillment
- Once having determined the buyer is qualified, relieve the pain—on your terms.

CONSOLIDATION PHASE

Step 7: Post-Sell
- Eliminate buyer's remorse and coach the now new client to deal with any fallout from the decision to purchase from you.

WHAT WAS THAT ABOUT PAIN?

The biggest piece of the buyer-seller "equality puzzle" (equal business stature with equal business respect) lies in uncovering the prospects compelling reason(s) to buy—what Sandler calls "pain." We talked about this in Chapter 1. Now you can see how it fits into the whole sales process.

Getting to a full understanding of the prospects' pain and what can potentially be done to help resolve their issues requires targeted, probing questioning and active listening. This is the secret to full understanding.

Pain, according to Sandler, is the gap between where prospects are and where they want or need to be. The bigger the gap, the greater the pain; the more pain, the higher the likelihood that prospects will be motivated to do something about resolving the issue. The more prospects feel their pain on an emotional (not just an intellectual) level, the more determined they will be to get it fixed quickly by someone who understands the significance/importance of the issue as well as empathizes with them.

How do you discover the full extent of prospects' pain and whether or not the primary pain associated with their issues is sufficient for them to undergo the secondary pain of having the pain reduced or resolved? That's right—by skillful questioning.

David Sandler transformed professional selling, armed with:

- His new behavior/attitude/technique model of success.
- A deep understanding of transactional analysis and the implications of how it applies to both buyer and seller, including Identity/Role Theory.
- A new model of the levels of pain.
- The expanded Sandler Selling System.
- An inquiring mind, which discovered the efficient and effective listening model, developed through intelligent, purposeful questioning.

All the basic elements were finally in place to transform the world of the buyer-seller interaction forever.

Sandler Training has since revolutionized the selling process down the decades and across the globe. Let's take a deeper dive in the following pages.

CHAPTER SUMMARY

- To succeed in sales, you must study and understand human interaction, motivation, and patterns of behavior.
- You must lead the Buyer-Seller Dance.

> *"The rewards for those who persevere far exceed the pain that must precede the victory."*
> —Ted Engstrom

CHAPTER 3

Walking though the Submarine

When David Sandler developed and refined all of the elements of his revolutionary sales process, he spent time looking for just the right metaphor to illustrate, illuminate, and help explain both the structure of the new process as well as the order/sequence of all of the primary steps involved. He eventually developed the Sandler Submarine—now familiar the world over to proponents of the Sandler Selling System, of course.

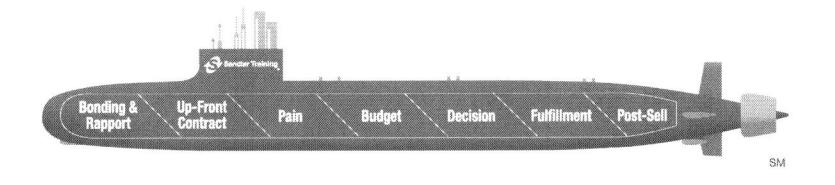

Sandler specifically selected the submarine metaphor to illustrate his new sales system because he thought that it explained to and reminded users how important it is to properly "'seal off'"

each compartment of the system before moving on to the next. That way, he encouraged proponents of his developing framework to make certain that absolutely nothing was left out before moving on. Sandler knew that, more often than not, it is exactly the hurried, forgotten, or omitted elements of any process that later come back to haunt salespeople if they have not properly dealt with them at the appropriate time. The principle here is a simple one. Whether you're undertaking a DIY project, fixing the car, creating a menu, playing chess, or selling a product or service, you get a better end result when you do two things: start well and follow a robust, clear, step-by-step process.

Still skeptical about that? Picture a submarine under a heavy and relentless depth-charge barrage. Imagine that in a moment of terror, the outer hull is breached right at the nose (for the landlubbers amongst us, that's the sharp, pointy end at the front).

Picture now high-pressure seawater flooding into the first compartment, with submariners running around shouting and desperately trying to seal the fatal gash with bits of bedding and wet clothing. Picture desperate red flashing lights, billowing smoke, and our handsome captain screaming blue murder trapped under a twisted gray metal girder with freezing cold water swiftly rising to chin level. If you can, also picture the crushing pathos of the camera zooming in to a shot of the battered teddy bear, Mr. Snuggles (given to him by his teary 3-year-old son at San Francisco harbor when the submarine left for war only two weeks before) floating by, just out of reach.

Well, there wouldn't be a dry eye in the house.

Now try to imagine that the dramatic music rises to a crescendo. By some heroic or superhuman effort, our handsome officer escapes from the grips of a certain watery death in the very nick of time—it's a nail-biter, no mistake.

To top it all, cut to a blood-stained hand reaching out to snatch Mr. Snuggles clean out of the icy water at the very second that three broad-backed sailors in clingy wet shirts heave closed the compartment door against the weight of the rising waters.

Phew. Disaster averted. I can hear the Oscar nominations being read out already.

Remember, that compartment is now completely flooded with icy water at thousands of pounds of pressure, and no one, under any circumstance whatsoever, is ever opening that door and going back in there again.*

SLOW DOWN

Many people know the old adage, "Less haste, more speed." Sandler recognized that way too often inexperienced and frankly shoddy salespeople who are so focused on the end result (the *yes* at the end that heralds the pat on the back and the fat commission check) that their better judgment becomes cloudy, making them scurry headlong toward the finishing line.

The prospect, however, feels the heat and the haste; he feels rushed, pressured, and harangued. If you have ever been on the receiving end of a desperate, pushy salesperson in a hurry to get you signed up or under contract with the new set of steak knives or driving away in the new car before lunchtime, you'll know exactly how awful that can feel.

David Sandler never wanted proponents of his selling system to make anyone feel that way—and his submarine ensured that the speed, pace, and rhythm of his system was better orchestrated by following the well-defined, step-by-step process that he developed.

---

* Even if someone left the remote for the TV in it.

EQUAL BUSINESS STATURE

The most important piece of the buyer-seller puzzle, the ongoing challenge that must surely have frustrated David Sandler most, was the issue of dominance and subservience—of power.

Sandler was not at all happy with the principle that the buyer was in a position of power and authority and the salesperson was in a position of weakness and servility. Sandler knew that for the buyer and salesperson to interact on an equal business footing, it was absolutely critical to achieve fairness and equality between them.

He realized that buyers always seemed to have a pretty robust buying system, whereas salespeople typically had none. The result, of course, was that invariably the relationship between the buyer and seller was stacked in favor of the buyer at the expense of the seller. The ultimate outcome was largely dictated by the rules and protocols of the buyer, while the seller (who had no system of his own to follow) became subservient to the buyer's wants, needs, and demands. Again, Sandler's new submarine model of the sales process gave those salespeople who could understand, internalize, and apply it a cast-iron sales framework to cling to—something to combat and neutralize the buyer's buying process.

We saw in Chapter 2 an explanation of the Buyer-Seller Dance. In absence of their own robust selling process, salespeople always have to defer to their buyers' process—they have no choice in the matter. Sandler knew that this was a bad state of affairs because if you don't know how to dance, who leads it? Here's a clue: It's not you!

The genius of the Sandler Submarine metaphor, therefore, gives you:

- A clear, operational, step-by-step sales framework.
- A mechanism that forces you to properly "seal off"

subsections of the sales process without missing any critical elements that might otherwise come back to haunt you later.
- A method whereby you can keep your momentum steady, low-pressured, and organized.
- A process to follow that allows equal business stature between salesperson and prospect.

In a single word, what the Sandler Submarine gives the world of sales is control. (To say nothing of a rather dramatic sea-rescue tale of heroism, derring-do, and Mr. Snuggles with which to regale your friends and family. Hoorah.)

Look again at the submarine.

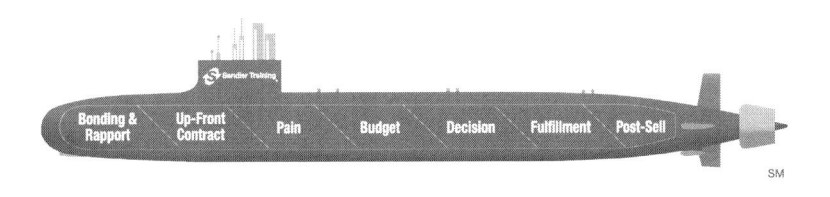

Notice again that each section builds on the framework and foundation of the previous one. It may seem obvious to us now when looking at the compartments that it's unlikely that the buyer will do business with you if he doesn't first feel some sense of affiliation or connection to you. Hence, you start everything with a powerful bonding and rapport framework. As you shall discover soon, this is much more sophisticated than a well-pressed suit, a big smile, and a firm handshake—in fact, it's quite the opposite.

It seems unlikely too, that people will part with their money if the budget issue hasn't been closely discussed and understood. Indeed, what salesperson worth his salt would make any kind of presentation to a prospect without first understanding what the prospect is able to commit to in terms of his investment in time, money, effort, energy, head space, and so on?

Spoiler alert: Most salespeople present their wares to prospects without first having any real understanding of any of the things above. They do so in the vain hope that the prospects will be so persuaded by the strength and sincerity of the salesperson's handshake and the compellingly cunning arguments and closing techniques, so impressed by the mastery and majesty of the PowerPoint skills being demonstrated, or so bowled over by the modernity of the cut of the salesperson's new and expensive Italian suit that all other concerns and apprehensions that buyer might be harboring will seem mere trifling piffles by comparison.

Or not!

THE SUBMARINE IN MORE DETAIL

The Sandler Submarine is so important to what follows in this book that you should become familiar with it. Let's take a few moments to examine how each of the compartments of the submarine work and the main elements and objectives of each.

Bonding & Rapport

Oftentimes, the opening Bonding & Rapport Step of the Sandler system, is called the "pattern interrupt." It is based on the principle that for a prospect to view you as *better* than your competitors, he first has to see you as *different* from them.

You can't be better than any of your competitors if you are not first seen as being different from them. You can't be better and the same.

Think about this for a second.

If you establish good early rapport with your prospect (and

continued rapport once he is a customer), it stands to reason that, all other things being equal, you are more likely to win and retain his trust and his continued business.

Consider this, too:

- People like people who are like themselves.
- People like to do business with people whom they like.
- Therefore, people like to do business with people who are like themselves.

If that's true (and it is), then successful salespeople's first job is to figure out what prospects are fundamentally like, and then quickly adapt their own behavior (body posture, tonality, language, volume, speed, attitude, level of OK-ness, reinforcement, etc.) to mirror and match those of the prospects.

Let's take a quick look at a prize-winning recipe for Bonding & Rapport.

Elements of Bonding & Rapport

1. You will need a strong sense of who you are.

Self-awareness is absolutely key. Before you can move to be like your prospect, you need to first understand who and what you are. A high level of self-examination and self-awareness is required. To determine how to get to where you want to go, you first have to determine your own starting point. Take time, dear reader, to understand your own point of view and level of emotional wellbeing, as well as your preferred methods and styles of communication.

As Socrates would have it, "Know thyself."

Confront some brutal facts; start by asking yourself some very probing questions.

- How do people see you? Is that different from how you feel you really are deep inside?
- If you won the lottery (and I mean *a lot* of money), where and how would you spend it? What is important to you as a person?
- Why are you in sales right now?
- If you died today, what would people say about you at your funeral?
- What do you most prize and value in life?
- If they made a movie of your life, would you be proud of what you saw?
- Are you a better person today than you were six months ago?
- If you lost all of your money tomorrow, what kind of person would you be a year from now?
- What are your best and worst qualities?
- How do you communicate?
- Are you a good listener?
- Do you express yourself clearly?
- Do you take time for others?

If you can have yourself professionally profiled or assessed, all the better. There are many reliable models on the market these days, and almost any reputable profiling organization will be able to give you real, measurable, and, most of all, objective data to consider. Your local Sandler trainer will be able to point you in the right direction. Contact the local office for more details. It is likely to be the best investment you have ever made for your future success.

2. You will need a highly-tuned emotional and situational radar.

To move to be more like your suspect/prospect/customers, you need to identify their characteristics and attributes—at speed. Successful salespeople have the ability to read the signs, feel the vibes, and pick up on the emotional state of the prospect. A highly-tuned and sensitive emotional radar is required. The best news is that it's like a muscle and can be developed and improved.

The most successful salespeople, like David Sandler, are real people watchers. They are hugely empathetic; they take time to observe, to listen, to explore, and to understand. Be like the psychiatrist, with your prospect on the couch. Sandler says that the art of sales is like a Broadway play being performed by a psychiatrist—to do this properly, you will need to really get inside your prospects' heads.

- How do they talk—loud, fast, quietly, softly?
- How do they think—in words or pictures?
- Are they self-centered or group-oriented?
- Are they talking tactically or strategically?
- Do they want it fun, fast, together, or right?
- Are they big-picture oriented or detail oriented?
- What's their mood? Are they feeling nervous, confused, embarrassed, indifferent, diffident, angry, hurt, jolly, excluded?
- How are they sitting, moving, gesturing?
- Are they visual, auditory, or kinesthetic?
- How does the prospect process information?

If you can match your behavior, actions, discussion, information, and so on with how your prospects understand the world, you will much more easily understand and connect with them.

Some people are visually oriented—working very fast, seeing everything in pictures, like a movie. "Show me this." "Let's see how that works." "I can see what you're saying." This kind of language provides the clues to watch out for—see what I did there?

Some people are oriented more toward processing information and understanding the world through what they hear. "I hear what you're saying." "Sounds to me like..." "If I'm hearing you right..." These are the clues to listen for. (I did it again, did you notice?)

Some people are more tactile. Statements like, "I get the feeling that..." "I'm sensing that you're telling me..." "That could fit..." and so on are what you want to notice if your aim is to stay connected with people in this group. (I did it again. I'm incorrigible, I know.)

3. You will need a good deal of style flexibility.

Now you have your starting point and you've observed where your prospects are. Next, you have to join them. The ability to move to where your prospects live is critical. If they are quick, you should be quick; if they are jolly, you should be a little jolly, too. If they are data-driven, you should verbalize matters in the same way; if they are reserved, pessimistic, or restrained, you should position yourself (and your argument) in ways that best align with your prospects' disposition and thinking styles. If they are thoughtful, you should position yourself to appeal to their considered approach. If they are data-nuts, don't tell them how you feel—show them charts. If they are concerned about the group, you should be able to illustrate how your proposition benefits the greater good; if they are only motivated by quick results, demonstrate with other successful examples how results have been achieved.

NOTE: You cannot expect them to move to be just like you; you have to do all of the work, I'm afraid. If one of you is exhausted after a meeting, it should be you. Prospects should always feel like you are the easiest person to get along with ever. You achieve that by making sure that you mirror their thoughts and behaviors, as well as their actions.

Style flexibility requires a large sense of professional humility as well as practice. Style flexibility is like a muscle—use it or lose it.

As counterintuitive as this sounds, you need to learn to be spontaneous. Plan being spontaneous first. Change your routines as often as you can. Embrace change. It is good—it will help you sell.

Try new things—all the time. Learn new skills. Practice, but in as many different ways that you can.

Question your thoughts and words—all the time.

Observe yourself. Ask yourself why you are doing what you are doing and why you are feeling the way that you are feeling.

Change the context—rearrange your physical and mental furniture.

Meditate—notice your physical and mental spaces.

Become a method actor. Recognize what it feels like to be happy, observe what it feels like to be sad, remember what it feels like to be calm. That way when you need to be those things in response to someone else, you can get there much faster and with much more conviction.

In short, you have to learn to be a social chameleon. Even a chameleon has to practice. "It's not easy 'being the twig,'" chameleons would tell you (I expect).

Professional Humility

Let's get something straight: Humility is not superficial hospitality, courtesy, or a kind and friendly demeanor that you maintain so you can "get down to business." It's an ongoing strategic choice you make in order to help others feel better about themselves.

In order to engage in this kind of strategic humility, you must stop believing your own hype. Turn down the volume of your mother's voice in your head telling you how amazing you are, how you are the center of the universe. Her loving and supportive voice built you up when you were small, but can stand in your way and stop you from going to the sales bank now.

Next, if you are going to appreciate another person's point of view, you have to be open. You have to be passionately curious about what's happening in the other person's world—more interested in that, believe it or not, than what is happening in your own world. Strategic humility requires asking questions about the other person out of genuine curiosity—so ask them. Lots of them!

Finally, to master professional humility, you really must get yourself a sales coach.

Think of anyone famous for any particular sport. Got one? Now think of two other successful people, each from a different sport. What three things, other than some innate quality that could be called "talent," do these people all share? I'll tell you. They all have a good, strong playbook, they all have a dedicated coach who knows more than they do, and they all practice, practice, practice. They don't practice until they get it right, they practice until they can't get it wrong. This is the essential difference between an amateur and a professional.

If you think that you know your job better than anybody else, that you don't need to practice, that no one can tell you anything, that you're just gorgeous and one of the universe's glorious sunbeams exactly the way you are, then put this book down and trot yourself off to a comfy seat and a steaming hot cup of tea in Mediocrity Land. That's where you are headed, and that's where you are going to stay.

Trust

Good, you're still here. Now you are on your way somewhere much better. But there's another little wrinkle here to consider—trust. Prospects not only need to feel that they like you, but they also need to trust you. Like and trust are not the same thing.

- There are people I like, but I don't really trust.

- There are people I trust, but I don't really like.
- There are people that I neither like nor trust.
- Then, there are people that I like and that I trust. Bingo!

You have probably heard of the adage, "People want to know how much you care before they care how much you know." It's one of life's biggest ironies that the single biggest thing that stands in the way of proper trust-building between salespeople and prospects is, almost always, the salespeople's inappropriate actions or mistaken beliefs.

When you are another salesperson's prospect, how do you feel? Intuitively, many people believe that most salespeople are out to fleece them—and that's why they don't trust them. The single best way to get prospects to trust you, therefore, is not to sound, look, or feel like a salesperson.

In other words, prospects have to believe that you (the salesperson) are able to put their interests above your own.

How do you do that? Make it all about them—not you and your company, your solutions, your USP, your secret sauce.

And, how do you do that? Ask better trust-based questions. Instead of saying anything remotely "sales-y," try saying something that is clearly not in your own self-interest. It's a great way to build trust very quickly.

Here are some examples.

"After I know a little bit more about your company and what you're trying to achieve, if I don't think I would be the best solution for you, would you be OK if I maybe suggested a couple of my competitors who might be a better fit?"

"So that I can be sure we are both on the same page: Other than price, which is always very important to all of my clients of course, what other criteria do you typically use when selecting new suppliers? If I don't believe we are going to be very effective in those key areas in, say, your boss's eyes, I'd rather tell you up front than risk any embarrassment for you later. Are you comfortable with that?"

"You know what, Susan, we are almost never the quickest in the market. If that's the single most important selection criteria for you, then I'd rather clarify that right up front and wish you well with your current supplier. If reliability is more important, however, then maybe we can talk. Does that sound fair?"

The Up-Front Contract

Wouldn't it be lovely, and in everyone's very best interests, if before a sales meeting (or a sales-discovery meeting), the buyer and the seller came to agreement on the following?

- The time, duration, and location for the meeting.
- The purpose of the meeting.
- The client's agenda.
- The salesperson's agenda.
- The potential outcomes of the meeting (what the next steps might look like if things were to continue).

Wouldn't it be even lovelier still if both the salesperson and the prospect agreed in advance that when they do meet, it's going to be important for both parties to ask and answer questions in equal measure?

And then, wouldn't it be top notch, in fact only a quick bus-ride from perfection, if both parties were big and brave enough to end the meeting with a very clear agreement to either continue the process or else stop wasting each other's time right then and there? Wouldn't that be the bee's knees, the cat's very pajamas?

Well, why can't it be that way? Why can't you agree on all of that critical stuff beforehand? Why can't you negotiate Up-Front Contracts with your prospects?

You can.

Look again at the quick list above. Then, the next time you're setting up a meeting, try these three magic set-up questions.

1. "So, Tom, exactly where and when would be best for us to meet?"
2. "Let's just agree on our top most-important items on the agenda. Is that fair?"
3. "Just so that we make sure that we are both on the same page, let's agree what the next steps might look like if we're a good fit. Are you comfortable with all that?"

Simple, right? Introduce these questions into your daily sales vocabulary today, and things will start to get better for you right away—even if you do nothing else new as a result of reading this book.

I'll share more on the benefits and power of up-front contracts later in the book.

Pain

Pain is the gap between where people are and where they want to be. Remember the genie from Chapter 1?

The first major role of the salesperson (after all of the bonding and rapport stuff), is to try to uncover the extent and depth of prospects' pain and to weigh it against the pain associated with the resolution that you might explore with them.

Think of this in terms of something most people can

understand: being a little overweight. It's easy to complain about not being able to still fit into whatever it was that you wore to your high school prom, but, until the day that the pain associated with losing those pesky excess pounds is greater than the emotional/psychological pain (discomfort, effort, energy, planning, time, head-space, and so on) with remaining overweight, many don't tend to do anything about it. Am I right? OK, let's agree to consider that a rhetorical question.

In this instance, the real and present pain associated with remaining overweight is (rhetorically speaking here) less than the pain associated with losing weight. So the pounds stick around.

If, however, the doctor tells a patient with a very solemn face that he is one more burger with large fries and a double strawberry milkshake away from a fatal embolism the size of a small SUV, the person is more likely to get himself down to the gym *prontissimo*. Suddenly, thanks to the MRI that shows in vivid Technicolor that he has enough life-threatening gloop in his arteries to lubricate a 747 jet engine, the pain associated with losing weight seems to pale in insignificance.

Let me add an extra wrinkle to the pain discussion. Sandler recognized that the issue that the prospect originally brings to the table is rarely, if ever, the actual issue that needs the real attention. What does that mean? It means skilled salespeople will have to get a pick and shovel out to do a little pain-mining. They have to transition their prospects from a surface-level pain to the richer vein of the real pain, one or two levels below. They have to take their prospects from a business-impact pain to a personal-impact pain.

Every sale is instigated by prospects in the belief (or hope) that they will feel emotionally better once the particular product or service is delivered and implemented. The trigger for the sale is entirely based on emotion. Pain is the single most compelling emotion leading to action. The ultimate decision to proceed or not is based on reason and is approved (or rejected) by the Adult and the Parent ego states, but the whole thing is instigated by the Child voice who wants all the needs met—now!

Sandler Pain Funnel®

- Tell me more about that...
- Can you be more specific? Give me an example.
- How long has that been a problem?
- What have you tried to do about that?
- And did that work?
- How much do you think that has cost you?
- How do you feel about that?
- Have you given up trying to deal with the problem?

Three Levels of Pain

Let me share with you a short scenario. A salesperson for Dust in Time, a local janitorial cleaning company, is meeting with a prospect, the principal of a high school, about possibly giving the company a try.

1. The initial/surface pain first mentioned

The principal tells the janitor that she's unhappy with the sloppiness of the work that her current cleaning company provides, and she would like a quote to maybe switch to a new company at the next semester.

The principal announces that she is seeing another rival company, too. So it's a competitive bid process. Therefore, a very competitive price will be required; the school is on a very tight budget.

The salesperson can either think, "Well, that sounds reasonable. I will get her my very best price and a glossy pack of literature out to her by the end of the day."

Or, he can engage his Adult-voice and ask a few probing/telling questions, such as:

- "Tell me a little more about what you have experienced—why are we even talking right now?"
- "What's the one thing that you wish were better with your current cleaning provider?"
- "What did the current company say when you told them that you weren't happy with their work?"

2. The second-level pain, as it relates/impacts on a business level

As a consequence of these initial probing questions, the principal somewhat reluctantly explains in a little more detail what has been going on. The salesperson starts to dig a little below the surface, getting closer to the real pain.

The principal shares that she has had a few complaints from the manager of the judo club who rents the gym on Wednesdays. One of his students cut his foot after slipping on a puddle on the floor, which hadn't been cleaned properly before the class started. She has also heard from another customer that rents the art room on Thursdays for a pottery class that there have been complaints about the cleanliness of the bathrooms.

The salesperson can either think again, "Well, that still sounds reasonable. I will get her my best quote and glossy literature pack out by today."

Or, he can ask a few more telling questions, such as:

- "How long has this been a problem for the school?"
- "What have you tried to do about it? Did that work?"
- "How much do you think that this has cost the school in lost opportunity or revenues—or threatened losses in revenue over the next few months?"
- "Has anybody else complained about this?"
- "What did the parents of the boy with the cut foot do/say?"

3. The third-level pain, as it relates/impacts on a personal level

By virtue of these more probing questions, the principal is now approaching the real pain. She goes on to explain that this kind of thing has been happening for much longer than she cares to think about, that the school board was really putting the pressure on to secure more and more additional revenues, that she can't afford to lose even one out-of-hours school rental, and that the current cleaning company has been told in no uncertain terms about the implications of these lapses—on numerous occasions—and it still hasn't done anything to rectify the situation. Enough is enough!

The salesperson can either think again, "Well, that still sounds reasonable. I'd be grumpy about it, too. I will get her my best quote and glossy literature pack out by suppertime."

Or, he can (and should) ask even more probing and telling questions, such as:

- "How much revenue do you think could be at risk if everyone that rents space from the school left at the same time?"
- "How would you feel telling the school board that everyone left and there was no more revenue coming in from classes because of the complaints about cleanliness?"

- "Have you given up trying to fix this?"
- "Would it affect your own performance review if the school were sued for injury to another student from poor cleaning execution?"

By digging down to the third level of pain, the salesperson has explored the initial surface issue; then the issues as they relate to the business aspect of the situation; and then right down to the fact that the principal is worried that her job might be at stake—and that would be a Child-based pain that she doesn't even want to consider.

What's more, the principal would go to quite some lengths (and investment) to execute a contract if she feels entirely confident that her new cleaning company (yours) will not put her livelihood at risk—in a role that she has worked hard for and that she deserves. And, no disinterested and incompetent vendor with low standards will take that from her!

I exaggerate to make the point, of course, but by asking the right pain questions and digging down from surface pain to business pain to personal pain, the prospect becomes truly emotional. Emotional people want their pain to be relieved by those whom they believe understand the significance of the issue and they trust to deal with it properly—you.

Budget

Let's look now at the fourth compartment of the submarine. There is a marked difference between a prospect who is willing but not able and a prospect who is willing and able. Perhaps you've even run into the occasional prospect who is able but not willing?

Successful salespeople need prospects who are willing and able to do business with them. With only one of the two (or worse, neither), it will be a real struggle to encourage any kind of prospect into gathering enough momentum to action—no matter how clever the sales close happens to be.

1. **Hint I:** If your prospects have neither the appetite (willingness) nor the means (ability), you're not going to get very much business from them. Don't forget to ask for the referral, though—always ask for a referral.
2. **Hint II:** The Sandler Budget Step is often called the "investment step" because there are investments that prospects need to make that often go beyond mere pounds/dollars/yen. For instance, time will need to be invested (by individuals, by whole departments, or even business at large). There's also the investment of effort; the investment of energy; the organizational head-space. There could be a requirement for widespread organizational change; there are habitual behaviors that may need reshaping (and they don't usually go down without a fight), and so on.

Some budget questions at this early stage might be:

- "What kind of investment were you expecting to make for this project, Tom?"
- "To use a hotel analogy, were you expecting to make a 1-, 2-, 3-, 4-, or 5-star investment for this, Jamie?"
- "Will you share with me the sort of range [or bracket, or ballpark] where this budget might start and then go up to in your past experience on projects like this, Sam?"
- "Were you hoping for 'good,' 'cheap,' or 'fast,' Alejandro, because you can't have all three?"
- "We all want the best value, Tadashi, but putting other things aside for the moment, what were you expecting to have to invest, in monetary terms only, at this stage?"

Decision

This is the last stage of the Sandler selling qualification process. After this compartment of the submarine, you will be able to:

Qualify the prospect to receive a detailed presentation.

...or...

Disqualify the prospect (in which case the person does not get a proposal/price/presentation).

...or...

Agree who else needs to be included in the sales process should it continue.

The salesperson should also understand and agree to all the timescales involved. By this, I mean the timescales for the presentation and those associated with the subsequent decision-making process.

A thorough Decision Step gives you a good understanding of when the decision will be made, by who (the cast of characters involved), where, how it will be made, and why it is that way. Armed with all of this information you can confirm that the prospect has earned the pitch. However, without a successfully completed Decision Step, you can expect a swing and a miss.

The Key Questions

Imagine that you're a reporter. You're just arriving at the scene of a large car crash involving, as far as you can tell, at least three cars, a firetruck, and a motorbike. As you jump out of your car and sprint over to where a policeman is pulling "Police: Do Not Cross" tape between traffic cones, what might you ask him? If you were going to be able to write up the report for the newspaper, you'd want to know:

- When did it happen?
- What happened?
- Where did it happen?
- Who is involved?
- Why did it happen?

Similarly, when you're at the Decision Step of your sales process, you need to take exactly the same approach you would if you were that reporter. Ask your prospects: **when** they would like to see the benefits of solution implemented, delivered, or in place; **what** exactly the presentation that you will be making should look like; **where** it will happen; **who** will be there (and what they each do); and, finally, **why** does it all have to be done this way?

Once you know the answers to these questions, you can decide whether or not to present the prospect with something at the next stage.

Fulfillment

Now that you have the trust and respect of your prospects, set up a clearly-defined process of cooperation and collaboration, developed a detailed understanding of the gap between where the prospects are and where they want to be, gotten a full understanding of the required investments (structural, conceptual, and financial), and identified the cast of characters involved in the decision tree, you can finally present something. Slide presentation time, right?

Well, possibly. But only if prospects are properly qualified to receive the proposal, and only if a slideshow is the very best way to get the message across. All too often they aren't, and it isn't.

Why? Because typically, this is exactly what the other guy is doing. As you'll see in a subsequent chapter, if your competitors are all zigging, you should do some zagging.

Consider this as well. If you don't like some of the answers you have heard along the way, or if you don't have a very clear view of what will happen next after the presentation/quotation, or if at any point you've gotten wishy-washy answers to ill-defined or weak questions, guess what? The prospect does not qualify for your proposal—even if you are super eager to present anyway.

Maybe you're eager to present because you believe the prospect is bound to be won over by the compelling strength of the sales presentation itself and the subsequent arguments from the bench you are prepared to offer the court.

Wrong!

If the prospect doesn't qualify for a presentation, you're giving unpaid consultancy and wasting everyone's time, effort, and energy—including your own.

NOTE (to self): Present less, sell more.

It should take a lot of high gates and tricky hurdles for the prospect to get to your good stuff (that is, your presentation/quotation/proposal/solution). You must protect and guard your good stuff. If you sell with real skill, the number and frequency of your quotations will appear to crash—but your conversion rates will skyrocket.

You know how you're always complaining that there simply aren't enough hours in the day to get all your work done? That's actually under your control. If you stop chasing rainbows that will never turn into business, you will have enough hours in the day. The better you get at recognizing those rainbows that don't lead to a little leprechaun and a pot of gold at the end, the better it will be for you.

As we have already seen, hope is not a high-growth strategy. Don't let yourself become addicted to "hopium." It isn't going to help.

There are many new questions to pose during the Fulfillment Step, too. This is not a case of show up and throw up. Your goal is not to throw the kitchen sink at the prospect, in the hope that something you might say might somehow attract the attention and pleasure of the audience.

The questions you pose now must relate only to the specific pains you have uncovered. Not only that, you must take the temperature of the audience all the way through the presentation. You must keep asking if each point you make is what people were hoping to see, and, ideally, get them to score you as you go along. This way you'll avoid those nasty surprises at the end of some fateful presentations when the buyer says, "Thanks very much, but don't call us, we'll call you."

Post-Sell

It's time to seal the deal, and more importantly, time to counteract any potential buyer's remorse.

Have you ever shaken hands on a deal, only to get back to your office two hours later to discover that something unexpected has gone wrong? A manager at your prospect's company, perhaps, has implemented a spending freeze; a work colleague has committed to an alternative plan, pipping you at the post; the owner has suddenly decided to "get involved" in the process. Buyer's remorse is a very real issue and needs to be addressed.

To help ensure this doesn't happen to you, Sandler recommends meeting it head-on. Take a deep breath and ask something like, "Can I tell you my biggest fear, Terri? I'm worried that I might have pressured you into this deal. Could that be true?" Questions like this must be employed before the contract is signed or the delivery/start date confirmed. These kinds of critical questions at this time either seal the deal or flush out possible reasons for backing out or roadblocks. This is not the time to cash the check and take to the hills.

Another important tactic is to rehearse the buyer on what to say to your competitors when they find out. Ask, "Alice, what will you say when [insert name of competitor] decides to drop their price at the last minute to buy your loyalty?"

Help prospects practice what to think and say when they get back to the real world—and their bosses, their partners, their spouses, or their former suppliers hear that they've given the order to you. All of those folks are definitely going to have something to say about this. You can't rely on their largesse or their sense of fair play. Nor can you rely on the strength of your new customers' commitment to working with you. They will need a good dress rehearsal. Give it to them.

Ask, "What do you think your boss [business partner, spouse, cat, city council member—or whoever is important] will say to you when you tell them that you've decided to go with us at this time?" Then ask a supplementary questions to this, "OK, and what will you say to that?" Then make sure that you help him to convince himself even more that you're the right solution.

Ask, "What would you like us to do next? What was the single most important thing that we have discussed that you're looking forward to most?" Finally, ask, "Why?"

Don't forget (this is the part most salespeople try to skip) the referral. Always ask for a referral, even if you've never worked with the prospects before. Yes, this will be uncomfortable the first time you do it. But if prospects have given you the order or go-ahead, they're the happiest and most optimistic they have been for a while. They expect great things—namely, their pain will be reduced or eliminated. That means right now is the perfect time to ask for a referral. Put on your grown-up shoes and ask, "Who else do you know or care about who could benefit from having a fresh pair of eyes looking over their [insert what you do]?" After that, ask, "What made you suggest that particular person?"

THAT'S IT—YOU'VE TRAVERSED ALL THE COMPARTMENTS OF THE SUBMARINE

Lovely. Lovely as a shared cookie. Even more lovely, in fact—lovely as two pieces of pie. Have yourself a celebratory piece of pie before you move on to the next chapter, and I'll do the same. Yummy.

CHAPTER SUMMARY

- If you qualify too easily, the sale is too hard. If you qualify hard, the sale is easy!
- Prospects have to earn your presentation.

> *"If you don't meet the standards, then you don't qualify."*
> —Harold Ford, Jr.

CHAPTER 4

Can We Agree to Disagree?

We saw briefly in Chapter 2 that having everyone on the same page of the songbook keeps the sales process tidy and zipping along at a good, steady pace. When prospect and salesperson have a shared vision and agreement on things, that massively increases effectiveness and efficiency (read: sales conversion rates). When prospects and salespeople don't have a fully-shared vision and understanding, Sandler describes this condition as being in a state of "mutual mystification."

That's not good.

If you have ever gone to a meeting with a prospect and what happened next took you entirely by surprise, it was probably because there existed a difference between what you were expecting and what the prospect was expecting. Whose fault was that, anyway?

If you said, "His"—nope. It was yours for not making sure to clarify these things ahead of time.

Why then don't salespeople always make sure that those things are clear and transparent, and why don't they go to great effort to get agreement with the prospect beforehand?

Well, proponents of the Sandler Selling System methodology do—and you should, too. Sandler salespeople frame commitments and agreements into questions. Below is an example of what it can sound like. Take time to make these questions fit into your world, and then start using them. You may want to actually write these key questions down, learn them, and then use them every day until they become habitual, natural, and conversational.

AN EXAMPLE

Let's pick up the thread when our Sandler salesperson has been talking to a new suspect on the phone, deciding whether he will become a prospect or not. (That's the first qualification hurdle, of course.*)

Our salesperson Julie is getting the feeling that she could possibly help the new prospect Mark, and a face-to-face meeting might make sense. She asks a question, of course, to determine whether her suspect will genuinely become a prospect or not—in other words, whether the two of them will take the next step together.

"So, Mark, it sounds to me like it might make sense for you to invite me over so that we can have a face-to-face meeting about the new manufacturing plant that you're planning. Is that fair?"

The key moment. Once she has asked that question, she must wait for his agreement. If she doesn't get that agreement, something is going wrong, and she needs to back up the truck.

---

* For more of this type of prospecting dynamite, see *Prospect the Sandler Way*, by John Rosso.

If Mark says, "No," to a face-to-face meeting (and it's OK if he does), then he isn't a prospect after all. Some will agree, some won't; so what? Julie should move on to the next suspect. The key words here are "invite" and "fair"—don't forget them, they are very powerful words. Use them whenever you can.

Let's assume Mark says, "Yes," or something that sounds like it. Julie says, "Fine."

Remember that word, "fine." Not, "great"; not, "awesome"; not, "I really appreciate it"; and definitely not, "Oh, that's just wonderful, thank you, thank you. Bless you—may prosperity itself bestow the graces of nature upon your house, and may you live a bounteous existence filled with sunshine, rainbows, and strawberry fruit tarts. May your children and your children's children know health, wealth, and riches beyond avarice." Get the idea? Absolutely no fawning or sycophantic words.

"Fine" is enough. Don't go over the top. Never go over the top.

"So, let me get my calendar out," Julie says. "Now then, let me see. When are you thinking, Mark?"

Another nice question. Let's pretend he says Wednesday at 3:00.

"All right. Wednesday, 3:00, you say?" Julie resists the temptation to appear too keen. Instead she asks, "If I can't make that, what would happen?"

Of course, there's a chance he'll say something like, "Well, if you can't make Wednesday at 3:00, it's all over. Wednesday or never; you decide." In that case, Julie will indeed decide—end of discussion. But he won't. He is far more likely to say, "If not Wednesday at 3:00, how does Thursday at 4:00 work for you?"

Remember—this is all about balance and control. Julie keeps the business status between the two of them level at all times. She agrees to 4:00 Thursday.

OK, she's in. Then she asks, "How much time are you putting in your calendar for that, Mark?"

Mark answers as most would. "How much time do you think we'll need?"

"Good question, Mark." Julie has just given her now-prospect a "stroke," or a positive message. Why not? People can never have too many positive messages, and it's a way to reward them for agreeing to the meeting. "Experience tells me that we will be able to figure out in maybe 10–15 minutes whether or not we are a good fit."

Nice. Mark is happy at that. Everyone likes short meetings.

"But," Julie continues, "if we're still talking after about 40 minutes, we'll probably want to begin the process of working out how we can do some business together. Is that sounding fair?"

Not too pushy from Julie. Notice the subliminal messaging.

"But, also," she says, "if I think that we can't help you out properly, will you be OK if I tell you as much? It will save everyone a lot of time and effort after all, right?"

Another nice question—it keeps Mark's level of OK-ness just right. He says, "Yes," to this—it's a universal *yes* question (see Chapter 13) that make him feel like he's in control. He will always say, "Yes"—so always ask it!

"Thanks. I guess it's only fair then that if at any time you don't feel that we are the kind of company you want to be working with, will you be OK telling me that, too? Don't worry, you won't offend me, and you'll still be on my Christmas card list, I promise."

Another universal *yes*. Try it.

"OK, fine. So let me get this straight: Thursday at 4:00, at your place, for maybe as much as an hour to talk about X, Y, and Z, correct?" Julie waits for Mark's agreement before continuing. "Super. Are you planning to invite any others to the meeting?"

If he says, "Yes," Julie doesn't just say, "Great, see you Thursday, ta ta!" No, she finds out who else is coming, what they do, and why he's inviting those people particularly.

By the way, if you want to be a Sandler Black-Belt Ninja with your portrait hung proudly on our Wall of Fame,* you would also ask to speak to those individuals before the meeting in an effort to get their agenda items as well as the issues that are most exercising their brains at the moment.

Let's get back to Julie.

"Just as a recap, Mark," she says, "typically we find that the best way for first meetings to go would be if I ask you a whole bunch of questions around the issue—you know, to try to see the business issue through your eyes. Are you OK with that?"

He won't say, "No," I promise. Hooray! Julie's prospect has just given her permission to ask questions. (Preview of coming attractions: It's very important that Julie remind him of this issue again when they do meet—but more of that later.)

"And, Mark, you're probably going to want to ask me a whole bunch of questions, too. Such as, who else do we deal with, how our processes work, what the timescales will likely be; you know, all of that kind of stuff, right?"

Now, I can all but promise you the typical prospect will be OK with this; if not, the salesperson shouldn't even be having the meeting. If the answer here is "no," back up and figure out what's going on by asking directly. (Gulp. Yes, do it.) But nine times out of ten, you're going to get a "yes." As did Julie.

She says, "Is there anything else you think we need to add to the agenda?"

---

* No, we don't actually have a Wall of Fame, but we could start one if you think it might help.

Good work. Splendid. He says, "No." Now, here's the magic.

"Great. And, just to be clear, Mark, what usually happens at the end of these first meetings is that once we know each other better, we can have a good feel for whether or not we will meet again or kill it; are you OK with that, too?"

He says, "Yes," of course. It's another universal *yes*.

"Fine. And if we kill it, I might even ask for a referral on the way out, but we'll get to that later, fair enough?"

Goodness, look how professional and forthright Julie is—very good. No mutual mystification here!

"OK. Well, if I don't hear from you and you don't hear from me, Mark, I'll see you Thursday at 4:00 for as much as an hour."

Bingo!

In the space of about two minutes, Julie:

- Asked a bunch of probing questions that gave her a better picture about what's really going on in her prospect's world.
- Gained a much clearer view of Mark's intentions and the strength of his real desire (or not) for any type of change.
- Obtained clear agreement to what the next steps look like.
- Set the relationship between herself and Mark at a healthy, professional (more equal) level.
- Introduced the concept that a *no* is perfectly OK and that she wouldn't be crushed if he has to go that route.
- Firmly differentiated herself from all of her competitors.
- Agreed at the beginning what the end might look like.
- Increased the effectiveness and efficiency of the next meeting.
- Clearly placed the prospect into the top of her selling process, not his buying process.
- Explained what doing business with her might look and feel like.
- Gave and gained permission to ask lots of questions.

All by asking very fair, easy to agree with, adult, non-threatening questions—very clever!

Beyond learning this script or something rather like it, what should you do? Perhaps take a moment to reflect on and consider what you have seen here.

What you've seen in this chapter is positioning. How was this accomplished by the salesperson? By asking good questions—principles and behaviors that the prospect agreed to, thereby entering into a contract ahead of time. At Sandler, we call this an up-front contract, remember?

We've seen an up-front contract (agreed to by inserting the right questions at the right time, for the right reasons) for the time, place, length, and subject matter of a first meeting. Up-front contracts can just as easily be used for many things in the selling world, such as:

- The terms and conditions of the next meeting, and then the one after that.
- What the elements of a price quotation or presentation might look like.
- What the next steps of the agreement are, and who is doing what, by when, and why.
- And so on.

Now, go back to the Sandler system you learned earlier. Consider what an up-front contract might look like, not just during the prospecting conversation but at every single step of the process: every time you meet the prospect again, and before you leave; every time you begin to speak on the phone, and then every time you say goodbye—every step of the way. What difference would that make? Considerable! My thoughts exactly. So, write yourself some good up-front contract scripts, use them, learn them, and watch the deals (and the money) come rolling in.

If you are typically a one-call close, you need one good up-front contact; if you are a two-call sales cycle, you will need two or three, and so on.

EMAIL ALERT

So, let's zip back to the face-to-face meeting that Julie and Mark have just scheduled. Let's imagine that Julie has just put down the phone. What's next? No, not a nice nap (though I do like your thinking). What happens next is a short email to confirm the agreement. It looks something like:

> Subject: Meeting: Thursday at 4:00
>
> Mark,
>
> I appreciate the invitation to meet to explore [insert issue].
>
> As discussed, naturally you're going to have a bunch of questions for me, such as: [insert three or four typical issues surrounding the issue].
>
> Obviously, as agreed, I'm going to need to better understand some things, such as: [insert three or four typical questions that you need to know answers to concerning the prospect's world, experiences, and history, and the issues].
>
> At the end of the meeting we will decide what the next steps will look like, and how to best proceed—even if it's a *no* at this stage.
>
> If you feel that you want to add to the agenda or invite anyone else, just drop me a quick note.
>
> Regards,
>
> Julie

NOTE: For full Ninja Sales Status and extra brownie points (and there's the Hall of Fame, that we're thinking about too, remember?), you will of course want to connect with your prospects' LinkedIn presence well ahead of time, too. Do some homework (due diligence) on them, their companies, and their interests, LinkedIn groups, college, previous roles, other connections, etc. Hey, no complaining. It's your job.

- Twenty minutes a day on LinkedIn, dear reader. It's important.
- Post every week, too.
- Get your LinkedIn profile just right—including a good photo.
- Keep your contact details updated.
- Link to your company website.
- Join LinkedIn groups as well.

Your next customer is on LinkedIn—remember that. Speak with a Sandler coach, who will help you set up LinkedIn and show you how to get it working for you. (See *LinkedIn the Sandler Way* for more on this vital topic at www.sandler.com/linkedinsecrets.)

OPENING THE MEETING

OK, so let's now imagine that it's Thursday at 3:50, and Julie has just arrived at Mark's office. Julie is waiting for Mark to collect her from reception. Julie has set herself some pre-call objectives. (Yes, really—it's what professionals do, remember? Pre-call objectives and post-call reviews are critically important to consistent success—"cold and hot washes," as the military calls them).

Before she arrived, Julie spent time on Mark's company website and learned about the business. She wrote down at least 10 great strategic and tactical questions to ask. She rehearsed and role-played the meeting out loud. (Salespeople's ears need to hear their mouths saying the words—the first time the director shouts, "Action," shouldn't be the first time the actor has a go at the script.) Julie is determined to have equal business stature with Mark, and she positions herself mentally for trying to understand whether there is a mutually beneficial relationship to be made.

Mark appears and beckons Julie through to his office.

In situations like this, before you launch headlong into your typical "weather and the price of fish" small talk ("Did you see the game last night?" or, "Is that your sailfish on the wall?" or, "Are those the grandkids? Lovely." Or, "Aren't we having an awful lot of weather lately?") this is a good time to stop and take a deep breath.

Why?

Because first, you want to slow right down. It's very important not to sound, look, or feel like every other salesperson out there. (When they zig, you zag.)

For Mark to see Julie as better than the others, he first has to see her as different. Remember, too, the sales watchwords—be curious, be skeptical, and don't be attached to the outcome. When you're in Julie's position, imagine that you're financially independent—you don't need the money. Act "as if."

Julie's first job is to take Mark's temperature, as it were, and then mirror and match what's going on. This is called bonding and rapport—but keep it brief, dear reader. If you're still working hard at bonding 15 minutes into a 45-minute meeting, you've overshot the target by quite some way. We recommend a maximum of 5 minutes in the Bonding & Rapport Step of the submarine. There's work to do, people.

Julie starts by setting the scene in terms of tone, professionalism, and expectation. Now is also the time to review the up-front contract that she made when she and Mark spoke on the phone.

"Thanks again for the invitation, Mark. How are things with you today?"

Say this with a warm smile. Learn how to get your tonality and Nurturing Parent voice just right; it's your most successful selling voice. Always use the word "invitation"; it's very strong. Be sure you use genuine tonality with your opening gambit. If you come off as snarky or insincere, it doesn't matter what words you use. Speak slowly, clearly, and with authority.

Once Julie has listened actively to Mark's answer and responded appropriately, the real work begins. Take a look at the below questioning structure and follow it as closely as you can. You should have prepared a pre-call plan, of course, with objectives for your call, along with appropriate probing questions (more on this later).

"When we spoke on the phone," Julie says, "we agreed that we would meet today to discuss 'x,' right? And we talked about how you would naturally be wanting to ask me lots of questions about how we do or deliver 'y,' correct? And, in order for me to be able to better see your world through my eyes, I would likely be needing to better understand 'z,' yes?"

Julie waits for Mark's agreement after every question, of course.

"We also agreed that by the end of this meeting we would likely realize whether or not we're a good fit, in which case either of us could say so without hurting the other's feelings, didn't we? But we also said that if we both believed that it would make sense to continue, we could agree to take things to the next level and agree on the next steps; are you still going to be OK with that? Finally, we said that we would meet today for up to an hour, and that we didn't need anyone else in the room at this early stage, correct? So, before we begin, has anything changed, or do we need to think about anything else right now? Great! Are you ready to begin?"

NOTE: Do not miss any steps from this important opening process. Each is critical to establishing equal business stature and collectively they remove the most likely roadblocks to your later progress. Get these early moves just right, and the rest of the sales process will be much, much more efficient for you.

These up-front contracts, supported by good questioning skills, are the single most powerful master key to the sales strongbox. Get into the habit of using this kind of language, these kinds of questions, the right voice, and Sandler's revolutionary sales process. There's money in them thar hills, par'ner.

CHAPTER SUMMARY

- The up-front contract is the single most powerful key to better sales success. If you get only one best practice from this book, it had better be this one.
- Asking organized and structured questions with the right tonality is the key to better up-front contracts.

> *"What all agree upon is probably right; what no two agree on is most probably wrong."*
> —Thomas Jefferson

CHAPTER 5

What Are You Trying to Say?

Human beings are extremely adept at picking up on tone of voice. The way something is said (tonality) is actually much more important than the actual words that are used. In fact, you can get the words exactly right, but if you get the tonality wrong, you're finished. On the other hand, if you get the words slightly wrong, but the tonality is just right, there's no harm done.

As we saw in Chapter 2 when we introduced TA (transactional analysis, remember?), there are three main ego states (voices): Parent, Adult, and Child.

Do you remember your parent's voice when, as an eight-year-old kid, you came hopping into the house in a flood of tears because you had just fallen off your bike and had skinned your knee? Your parent probably adopted a voice that soothed and helped you out. The voice said, "There, there," patted dry your tears, and put a bandage on the offending knee, and gave you a drink of warm milk and a big, safe cuddle. It was a good voice. It was a reassuring and gentle and kind and helpful voice. It was a safe voice. You guessed it. It was a Nurturing Parent voice.

The Critical Parent voice, however, is the voice that you heard when you were 16 and came in late after curfew and didn't call ahead to explain. Think about that voice right now. That's probably not a good voice to use in a sales environment.

The Authoritative Parent voice is the voice that said that yes, you could have friends come around, but not until your room had been tidied like you agreed, young man. Again, not a good voice to use in a sales encounter.

You always have to be intensely aware and consistently mindful of which voice you are using and why—not only during the actual sales calls, but in emails, voicemails, presentations, and quotations, too. The Nurturing Parent voice should be your default sales voice. It speaks to the frightened and concerned Child in your prospect and makes it feel understood and safe. At least 70% of your selling voice is Nurturing Parent.

Of course, there are times when the voice you adopt should be the Adult voice; when facts, figures, and logic are the only way to make your prospect's own inner Adult voice comfortable enough to continue.

Sometimes, it should be the Child's voice that comes out of your mouth, mainly in the bonding and rapport portion of the meeting near the beginning and near the end only. This sounds like lighthearted small talk—but don't do too much of it.

If ever you find yourself mired in logical, reasonable, rational, sensible discussion with prospects, it's likely they are in their Adult and non-emotional/entirely rational ego state. Respond to this by asking the right questions to bring out their Natural Child. Ask their inner Child if it wants to come out to play. The Child lives in an emotional state, so bring it out by asking emotionally charged questions.

- "Let's pretend that we could get this fixed for you. How might that feel?"
- "Let's imagine that we could do this for you. Would that be a good thing?"
- "Patricio, if you had a magic wand, what would you wish would happen next?"

Who runs around pretending, imagining, and waving magic wands? The Child, that's who.

This mechanism serves to have your prospects quickly drop down a gear into their Child ego state so that you can get past the logical and authoritative gatekeepers in their heads and find the real issue, the real pain.

Then, be sure to sound incredulous and concerned. Engage your Nurturing Parent voice (it's all in the tonality, remember?).

- "How did that make you feel?"
- "Has this been happening long?"
- "What have you tried to fix it?"
- "Is it still worrying you?"
- "What did you think when you heard that?"
- "Doesn't that kind of thing make you angry?"
- "Didn't that upset you, even a bit?"
- "I bet you couldn't believe it."
- "No way."

Get the idea?

Get your prospects/clients thinking and talking about the issue on an emotional footing, then empathize with them (nurturing voice) and keep them OK by being slightly less OK than they are (otherwise you force them back up into their logical thinking mindset). The longer you keep your prospects' Child voice active, the more pain you can discover and the more likely they will insist that you're the very best person to put the bandage on their hurty knee.

THE SUCCESSFUL QUESTIONING MODEL

To succeed in your new questioning approach to selling, you need a model to keep you on track. Here now is the essence of effective "selling by questioning."

Confidence
Outlook
Responsibility

ATTITUDE

SUCCESS

TECHNIQUE

BEHAVIOR

Goals
Plans
Actions

Strategy
Preparation
Focus

- **Behaviors** of effective questioning: These are the practical applications and circumstances you will need to create and the correct responses to them.
- **Techniques** of effective questioning: This refers to the construction, classification, and types of questions, as well as the specific words to use (and not to use) when trying to get to the reality of the prospect's situation.

- **Attitudes** of effective questioning: This means understanding your rights in the sales process. It means taking responsibility for who is in charge of the interaction, who is there to ask and answer questions, and how best to get to the truth.

There have been many long debates concerning which of the three elements of the Sandler Success Triangle model are the most important: behavior, attitude, or technique. When I first made this same inquiry of my Sandler master (well, coach, but "master" makes him feel a bit better about himself, so why argue), I was met with, "Ah, my young, inquiring and devilishly handsome student,* which of the three legs of a three-legged stool is the most important? Which of the elements of fire are the most important: the heat, the oxygen, or the fuel?"

"Errrr, I don't know," I replied.

"That which is missing, young Skywalker,** that which is missing," came his rather gnomic reply.

Here's an example. On May 6, 1954, at Iffley Road track in Oxford, England, Roger Bannister ran a sub-four-minute mile—and it changed the world.

Prior to this momentous event, physicians the world over had maintained that the human frame was incapable of running a mile in less than four minutes. Scientists, doctors, neurologists, professors, sports scientists, athletes, and so on, believed, understood, and agreed with absolute certainty that is was impossible to do so—not improbable, but genuinely impossible. This was an unquestioned and unambiguous biological and neurological fact. It was believed with 100% complete conviction that since

---

* I'm not exactly sure he used those very words, but they were on the tip of his tongue I'm sure.

** Again, I'm not positive he actually called me that, but it adds to the romance of my memory of it, so let's just pretend that he did, OK?

the dawn of time, humans had never, nor would they ever, achieve this immense feat—impossible, no matter what manner of hairy, sharp-toothed, and slavering ravenous fleet-footed wild beast was in pursuit with an evil glint in its eye and a desperate rumbling in its tummy.

A mile in less than four minutes was just plain impossible.

Yet, somehow, on May 6, 1954, a young British university student did it—in three minutes and 59.4 seconds.

What's more, Bannister was not a professional athlete—he was a student, back in the day when all one did as a student was, well, be a student. He didn't have professional coaches refining the separate elements of his running style. He had no nutritionists looking after his diet. He had no global brands sponsoring his "second skin, designed in a wind tunnel" running gear. He didn't have a specialist in the gym designing his weight-lifting regimes or medics measuring his glucose and red-cell levels on a daily basis.

So, how did Bannister do it?

Perhaps more importantly, how was it that with millions of years of evolution, not one single human being in the history of ever had ran a mile in less than four minutes, until Roger Bannister achieved it? How did the next person beat Bannister's new record only a mere 45 days later? How about within months, the dozens like him? What on earth had changed?

Belief. Conviction. Attitude.

Bannister, and all other runners the world over, knew well enough how to run (technique); they practiced a lot, tried to eat well, and got lots of sleep (behavior). Yet the sub-four-minute mile record remained intact. All runners the world over also believed (attitude) that it was impossible to cross that mythical time barrier. That is, until someone did it; then all bets were off.

Nowadays high school kids run sub-four-minute miles all over the place.

And guess what? The world is simply littered with such stories. Here are a few.

They said it was impossible for a human to conquer Mount Everest without portable oxygen tanks. And it was, until Reinhold Messner did it in 1978. Now if you climb Everest with supplementary oxygen, you're considered a little bit of a sissy! A 13-year-old boy has even done it.

They said that heavier-than-air powered flight was impossible. And it was, until Orville and Wilbur Wright decided that it wasn't.

It was impossible to split the atom, until Enrico Fermi decided that actually it wasn't.

Impossible for the blind to read? Louis Braille didn't get that memo.

It was simply impossible to walk to the North Pole (or maybe not); to break the sound barrier (oops); to see through solid objects (errr); to cure polio (done); to talk to people in other countries (yep); to build a bridge that spanned 100 feet; to fertilize a human egg outside the body; to dig a tunnel under the ocean; to see into an atom, to [insert your own personal myth]; and so on, and so on, and so forth.

So, dear reader, my submission to you is this: Bannister knew how to run, Messner knew how to climb, and the Wright brothers knew that birds could fly and that they were heavier than air. They all believed that the impossible was doable. They had unshaking belief—conviction. They had a winning attitude.

"Impossible" is not a fact; it's just someone's belief.

DETERMINATION DETERMINES THE WINNER

Asking good questions requires the right attitude. And yes, just like developing a muscle, the more you do something, the better you get at it.

What is it that allows you to ask the prospect difficult questions?

What is it that allows you to plant your feet and not let prospects lead you in a merry dance of "quote and hope"?

What is it that allows you to say to a prospect, "Well, I'll do that for you, if you can do this for me"?

What is it that drives you outside your comfort zone to stretch and try new ideas and practices?

What is it that makes you make just one more call, send one more email, ask for one more referral, ask one more question?

What is it that makes you feel better about giving than taking?

What is it that drives you to run the race faster than you ever thought possible?

A winning attitude—that's what you need.

You need to develop your winning-attitude muscle by starting to believe the following kinds of statements:

- "I have the right to prospect in my market."
- "I have the right to ask the difficult questions to get to the truth."
- "My customer and I are on an equal business footing—we have equal business stature—and that is reflected in the questions that I ask."
- "I am determined that I will succeed, and I will."
- "I believe in my sales process, and I believe that asking questions is better than giving answers."
- "Today I will break through my comfort zone and stretch the boundaries of my capability."

- "I will have a call plan written down before I go into the meeting with a range of questions prepared ahead of time."
- "To best help my client, I have to get to the truth; to get to the truth, I have to ask better questions."
- "Every day I get better at what I do—every day I ask better questions."

Everyone knows how to build muscle—repetitions and increased weights over time. To build muscle memory—rote and repetition. To build skill—practical application, intentional practice, and relevant experience. To build learning capacity—conscious, applied inquiry, and study.

The same is true of attitude.

"Wait a minute, Antonio," you might be saying. "Are you trying to tell me that the more effort that I apply, the more that I practice in an organized and targeted way, the more conscious the application of that learning, the more experience I have, and the stronger my belief system is, the better I will actually get at something and the more likely I will be to change myself, my circumstances, and, by extension, the world?"

Err, yes!

"Does this apply to questioning skills?"

Yes!

"Does this apply to professional sales?"

Yes!

"Well, shouldn't I get started then?"

Yes, please! Off you trot.

Do what Roger Bannister did. Get your attitude right. Once you do, it will become clear to you that it's OK to ask people questions—lots of them. As soon as you believe that, in your gut, 100%, things will change significantly for the better in your career—and your life.

CHAPTER SUMMARY

- Find out who's really talking, then ask questions that allow you to nurture, nurture, nurture.
- The winning attitude is all in your head.

> *"It's what you choose to believe that makes you the person that you are."*
> —Karen Marie Moning

PART 2

The Truth Will Set You Free

OK, so what next?

In Part 1, you learned the critical importance of having a selling system to counteract the buyers' buying system.

You learned, too, that while the buyer and the seller often have conflicting approaches, the control and level of business stature should remain on an equal footing of mutual respect.

You were introduced to the concept of pain and began to understand levels of OK-ness. You learned that tonality in the sales arena is as important as the words you use and that questions are the secret to greater clarity and better understanding.

You explored the TA voices that are at play in every human interaction.

You heard about the fact that success lies in three critical areas (behaviors, attitudes, and techniques) and that having the right attitudes and beliefs allows you to plant your feet, to get your head screwed on straight, and to question more effectively.

In Part 2, you will explore what it takes to differentiate yourself from your competitors, how to get your prospects' attention, and how to form an agreement with your prospects regarding joint expectations. All of this is essential to good questioning.

Also—spoiler alert—I will introduce you to one of the biggest sales secrets of all time: How to succeed in sales by getting permission to ask questions.

Let's keep going!

CHAPTER 6

When They Zig, You Zag

There are two kinds of people in the world: proactive and reactive. In the first group are those who look after themselves (who eat well, drink in moderation, don't abuse tobacco, exercise regularly, look after their cholesterol, and so on). In the second group are those who don't do these things.*

Regardless of which category you think describes you best, I'd like you to consider something. Before humans make any substantive conscious change, they first must have an internal dialogue that sounds something like this: "OK, friend, it's just you and me. We're in this together. We've got to get this thing done right. Maybe there are a few tricks that we haven't picked up yet. Maybe my saw could do with a little sharpening."

---

* Or at least they don't until the very second that they find themselves at the business-end of a defibrillator and promise solemnly to their god (and to any others that might be listening) that if they help them through the next 30 minutes they will be reformed, rejuvenated, and calorie-counting characters who will eat better, get more sleep, and do wondrous and remarkable deeds for humanity as a whole.

As Woody Allen once said, "If it's not one thing, it's your mother."

From their very first smile to their first cleaned plate; from their first faltering steps to their first words; from their first colored picture where they stayed within the lines to the first time they dressed themselves; from their first day at school to their clean hands before dinner—children have all heard how wonderful, clever, resourceful, and talented they are. They heard how proud they made Mummy and Daddy. They heard how they were the very embodiment of glorious deliciousness.

If the typical parental response to a first report card was anything to go by, every grade-schooler could almost certainly leap tall buildings in single bounds if they would just put their minds to it.

So why then isn't that Nobel Peace Prize sitting proudly, this very second, on the mantelpiece? Why isn't everybody a captain of industry? Why doesn't everyone have a day in the calendar devoted to them? Why, in this vast and wide world of opportunity, are they not building statues in everyone's likeness?

Let me start with the bad news—you had better sit down for this one.

News flash: You're not the smartest, cleverest, most beautiful, or talented person that was ever born. Truth be told, you may be like me—a good face for radio that could do with a wash.

"You mean to say that my mommy, she—she—lied to me?" you implore between horrified sobs.

Well, maybe your parents didn't exactly lie to you, but they did mislead you a bit. Maybe they actually believed it. Unfortunately, they were wrong. There, I've said it—it's out there. Go have a glass of water and a quiet sit down in a darkened room for a few minutes while you compose yourself.

IT'S NOT THEIR FAULT

Parental intentions are beautiful, of course. They love their children with all their chubby, gurgling life. It's not their fault; they are biologically predisposed to support, defend, and protect you. They meant every single word. Yes, when they called little Dylan, who had just helped clean away the dishes after dinner, "the kindest, most helpful child in all of creation," they meant it. They said it, they meant it, and little Dylan believed it.

This served to make Dylan extremely keen to curry favor with the parental units—to do things that elicited positive attention, praise, and reward from those in charge.

Then, to make matters worse for poor deluded Dylan, the whole of formalized education piled on to encourage even more socially integrated compliance. Learn this, don't learn that—the rewards will be significant. Behave this way and not that way—you'll get along. Appreciate this, think that, understand this, ignore that, give this, take that—and on and on.

Many people grew up programmed through positive and negative reinforcement to believe that certain behaviors and actions were inherently good: speaking when spoken to, looking for support and affirmation from those in authority, answering questions as completely as possible, being the smartest person in the room, having a good career, not discussing money, not talking to strangers, and so on. All of that was desirable, accepted, expected—normal, if you will.

Later, by hook or by crook, by plan, design, or happenstance, some found themselves in the commercial selling environment. They became sellers for a living: to bring food to the table, to pay the mortgage, and to put shoes on their children's feet. They became desperate, in other words—and that's when the professional problems began.

Everyone knows (including the prospect to whom you're trying to sell) that prospects are in charge and it's the salesperson's job to agree to the prospects' demands. Right?

Isn't that what you've been programmed to think? To see prospects (and others who control money decisions) as the authority figure in the relationship? To do what they ask, to comply, and to accept that their version of the truth is the only one that matters?

Guess what? When you follow that programming, the prospects are in charge—they are in control. Salespeople are conditioned to comply to the wishes and whims of their prospects. They want to gain that approval—just like at home and just like at school.

In a nutshell, when this programming is influencing you, you're desperate for prospect approval and they are in charge—a recipe for "do as you're told" if ever there was one.

And, just like when Mummy said, "You'll sit there until you eat that beetroot, young man," you did it because she was in charge. Let me repeat: People were programmed to do what they are told by those in charge. In the sales arena, the prospect is in charge. Right?

Wrong! You have just as many rights and just as equal of a business stature as your prospects and customers.

Gulp!

BRAVE LITTLE SOLDIERS

First of all, everyone reading this is going to have to be brave little soldiers. This is going to be a scary journey, there will be times when you want to give up and times when your family, your prospects, your work, your boss, or your bank manager will think you unhinged and encourage you (in the strongest terms) to stop acting so erratic, stop asking so many questions, and go back to what you were doing before. That is when you will know for sure that you're on exactly the right path. Take heart, young sales warrior, steel yourself, and be prepared.

If something is worth doing, it's worth doing reasonably well, at least. If you're going to be a bear, be a grizzly, right? Determine right now that you're going to change the game—and change the outcome. You're going to do something that "interrupts the pattern." You're going to not do what everyone else in your industry does. You're going to treat prospects and customers differently—and they are going to treat you differently in return.

When everyone else zigs, the best thing you can do is not to zig. You need to be different, special, memorable, noteworthy—you need to zag!

This does not mean blind and mindless change for change's sake in some sort of random, hopeful, and naive way. As with everything else, you need a plan, a strategy, and a measure of what "good" looks like, as well as an understanding of which milestones along the way will indicate whether or not you are making the difference you want to make. Your aim is to make the right difference at the right time for the right reasons.

Believe me when I assure you that the very last thing you want to look, sound, and feel like is every other salesperson with whom your prospects deign to meet. Some things are going to have to change. Also, it's true that the last thing your company wants to do is look, feel, or sound like every other marketplace competitor of yours.

POP QUIZ

What's so special about trying to be seen as different anyway? Why should you try so hard to be different?

Well, here's my wish for you—I wish that your prospects will soon come to view you as a trusted advisor, a person to be reckoned with, a confidant, a consultant—someone with equal business stature to them. Don't you want this for yourself? If you do, then you are starting right now on the road to more money. There are many vendors with whom you compete, many options that your buyers have. There are few trusted advisors, however.

The question is: How do you correct the disparity between where the prospect typically sees you and where you truly deserve to be—on the same level?

As was said before, to be perceived as better than your competitor, your prospect first has to see you as different from your competitor. You can't be better and the same.

The "same" is:

- Asking, "Please may I? Please can I? Should I? Could I just…" a lot.
- Saying, "I'd be happy to send you a quotation," whenever asked and not charging for it or getting any recognition in any way whatsoever that you've just done the prospect/client a huge favor that should be remembered but won't be.
- Saying, "Of course, you can think it over. Shall I call you next week?," and then not getting too despondent or grumpy when the prospect appears to have joined the Witness Protection Program when you call.
- Saying, "Let me ask my manager if we can look at the price/delivery/rebate for you," because, "No, sorry," or better, "What would happen if I do?," might offend.
- Saying, "I'm not very good at discussing money," to yourself a million times a day and then caving 20% on the price when the prospect so much as flickers an eyebrow when hearing the quotation/price.

- Saying, "I'm sorry to bother you, but…" or other such fawning nonsense that confirms that you don't see yourself as anywhere near the top of the food chain.
- Saying, "I hope this isn't a bad time, but if it is, I'm so sorry to have bothered you, your highness. Shall I go and wait in my basket in the corner of the room?"
- Asking, "Would you prefer next Wednesday or next Thursday?" or any such other tired, old, predictable, vacuous sales closes.
- Smiling too much. Being too jolly. Laughing too loud. Shaking hands too forcibly. Being too awesome—all the time, like you've just graduated from Bobo's Clown School. (You'll be making balloon animals for them soon if you're not careful.)
- Saying, "No, no problem, at all; I'd be glad to get that to you by [insert unfeasibly impossible and unrealistic timescale]," like it's your duty to stop the world while your prospect's needs are met. Your needs? Oh, don't bother with those. You're in sales, after all. You chose the job, not me.

If any of that described your current pattern, that's why you get treated the same as everybody else—you are the same as everybody else. If you continue to do what you've always done, you'll continue to get what you've always got. If you want the output to be different, the input has to change. That means you. You have to change. Doing more of the old behavior does not get any new results.

A DIFFERENT DISCUSSION

Let's imagine that you are an auto-insurance salesperson. Let's imagine I am a new customer. Let's imagine that we met at a lovely $10 networking opportunity, and I let you know some details about my policy. Here's what you don't want to say at the end of our meeting:

> "Thanks for your business, Antonio. If you ever need anything, you know where I am. Talk to you in April. Oh, just before I let you go, don't forget to tell your friends and neighbors all about our Introductory Special—a $25 voucher to you for everyone that you recommend to me that gets a policy within the next 60 days in auto or home insurance with my preferred carrier if over $500, but not including tax. I'll email you a leaflet, OK? I really appreciate it. You're the best. Thanks, bye."

That's the same.

This is different:

"So, Antonio, that's all the paperwork finalized. Anything else you need right now?"

"No, I think that's everything."

"OK, good. A last question or two. Antonio, you've probably noticed that I haven't asked you for an introduction over the last few weeks while we've been getting your policy to bed. That's because I never want you to feel that I'm being pushy or demanding, know what I mean?"

"Sure."

"So, with all of the uncertainty and turmoil that I'm seeing in the industry over the last couple of years and how frustrated people are getting with premiums going up and coverage going down—as well as clients getting grumpy about poor customer service and blockages in claims from some of the larger carriers—would it make sense for you to think about someone you care about who might benefit from a fresh pair of eyes reviewing their policy for them, too? Is that fair?"

If you're in the insurance world and are not asking something just like that to every single one of your current and lapsed customers every single day, well, you should be. Start doing so, immediately.

If you're not in the insurance world, figure out your killer referral question, too. There's money in that question—lots of it.

Let's agree to start asking for referrals—every single day—in a wholesome, honest, and aboveboard Sandler kind of way.

Let's also agree to a few other things, right now, too.

- Let's agree to plant our feet and not cave at the first sign of resistance from suspects, prospects, or clients.
- Let's agree to grow a backbone and stand our ground when prospects demand too much of us with no promise of anything in return.
- Let's agree to start to earn the money that our professionalism, experience, and expertise deserves.
- Let's agree to stop sounding, feeling, or looking like all of the other competitors' salespeople out there.
- Let's agree to be an active participant in our own futures.
- Let's agree to stop relying on hope—hope is not a high growth strategy.
- Let's agree to ask for referrals—all the time.
- Let's agree that when it all gets difficult and feels safer the old way, we won't cave at the first speed bump. A habit takes a little while to form (25–30 days—not long, really, in the whole complicated scheme of things), so give it chance.

- Let's agree to poke our heads above the parapet, take a big breath, and actually change something. Let's stop zigging and start zagging.
- Let's make a solemn promise with ourselves that today is the day.

I'm now hoping that you've had the internal dialogue that sounds something like, "You, know, he might be right. This might be just the very thing for which I've been waiting and looking. In fact, you know what? He is right and I am going to change. The current situation isn't good enough. I do deserve better."

Good.

So, where to start?

Start by learning to ask the right questions for better understanding and to show the difference between you and the rest of the pack. Asking good questions differentiates you and, as an added bonus, helps you to figure out how your prospect wants to buy from you.

Trusted advisors ask really smart questions. Vendors answer dumb ones.

CHAPTER SUMMARY

- To your parents, you were the center of the entire universe. They had your best interests at heart. But as to the rest of the world? Not so much.
- For your prospects and customers to see you as better, they must first see you as different.

> *"Be different so that people can see you clearly amongst the crowds."* —Mehmet Murat Ildan

CHAPTER 7

You Have Your Prospect's Attention—Now What?

Once you have your prospect's attention, then what? Simple. Ask a question, then shut up.

I mean it. It's time to explode the myth that the best salespeople are the best talkers. Stop talking about your features and your benefits and all the other boring stuff they dumped on you during product training. Instead, start asking smart questions.

As we have seen, one of the best ways not to sound, look, or feel like every other salesperson is to stop answering questions and to start asking them—to stop talking and to start listening.

Talk about zigging when everyone else is zagging!

BEYOND THE BLARNEY STONE

Supposedly, good salespeople have the gift of the gab—a touch of the old Blarney Stone, as they would say in Ireland. You know the kind of person I'm talking about—a "natural speaker," a "real communicator," the one with the ability to talk the hind legs off a donkey.

The truth is, however, these folks are not good salespeople. They just talk a lot. They spend hardly any time at all asking questions. (On those rare occasions that they do, they are unlikely to listen to the answers.)

The worst thing about these kinds of salespeople is that they make buyers feel like they're being sold to, and absolutely no one likes that feeling. Yet for some salesperson, the need for (their parents') approval is so high and they are so keen to demonstrate how much they know, their mouth stays permanently in overdrive, their brain in neutral, and their ears on vacation.

This is a major problem. Whenever buyers feel that they're being sold to by salespeople, they naturally try to protect themselves. They—how to put this politely so as not to offend—sometimes don't tell the truth, the whole truth, and nothing but the truth. OK, the truth is: They lie.

You do it, too. Admit it. When you are someone else's prospect, you probably lie as well. It's all about the attempt to keep control of the buying process; to keep the upper hand; to keep something in reserve; to keep your cards close to the vest; to keep the salesperson off balance; to keep yourself in charge; to make the salesperson work for that commission. In short, you lie to protect yourself.

Guess what? When you are the seller, the buyers lie right back to us, too. Gasp! The horror! I know.

Proponents of the Sandler Selling System recognize that in the typical buyer-seller relationship, the balance of power is all wrong. Buyers believe that they are in the position of dominance (the position of power, the position of control) and that the salesperson should be passive and subservient to them. Truth be told, even non-Sandler salespeople know this. It's the way of the world.

Mark Twain said, "What gets us into trouble is not what we don't know. It's what we know for sure that just ain't so." Dear reader, the buyer ain't in control unless you want it that way—and you shouldn't want it that way.

In any business exchange, you need equal business stature. That starts in your head. If you allow your prospects to be in control, they will be. If you allow your prospects to be dominant, they will be. If you allow yourself to be servile, you will be.

The easiest, quickest, simplest, and most powerful way to shift the balance of power is to ask more questions. If you want to be seen as the consultant, act like one. Ask good questions!

Let's go back to when you were the lackluster insurance salesperson. Remember, you and I met at the $10 networking event. I happened to mention that my car insurance was up for renewal soon.

Here's what the conversation might look like (and yes, I exaggerate here to make a point or two—so no letters to the publishers, please).

"Well, thank goodness that we met this evening," I say. "Tell me, why should I consider using you or your company for my car insurance needs right now?"

"Well, I don't know," you reply. "Maybe you shouldn't."

"Oh? Why not?"

"I guess the best way to describe it would be that our clients are quite—selective, serious, and discerning. We're not for everyone. Do you know what I mean?"

How about that as a strong and unexpected (pattern interrupt) opening line?

Use your Nurturing Parent voice, please (being careful not to use the Critical Parent voice).

Doesn't this feel somewhat better as a sales posture than what a person is used to hearing? "We've been in business a million years. We try very hard. I will do my very best to keep you happy, right up to the moment that I get your check; then I'll disappear. We always undercut the competition, but I sometimes forget to mention that our coverage isn't quite as good as your old policy. But it is $5 cheaper."

Let's go back to, "Maybe you shouldn't." Aren't the best prospects (the ones who you honestly do want as clients, the ones who have money to spend, the ones who are likely to be a little discerning) going to hear what you say and think to themselves, "Well, why can't I be in that exclusive club, too? I'm as good as the next person—better even. What's so special about this insurance? I bet this salesperson really looks after the clients. Why can't I play?"

Hear how the Child is engaged, intrigued, interested, eager to join in?

The conversation continues.

"We're not for everyone. Do you know what I mean?"

"I guess."

"Of course you do, of course you do. Our clients have already figured out for themselves where all the money comes from for their multi-million dollar Super Bowl halftime ads, right?"

"Oh sure, Super Bowl ads."

"The poor overcharged policy-holders, like you."

"I guess. Probably."

Engage your Nurturing Parent voice now, please—then keep it that way.

"And, do you know what else?"

"What?"

"Well, we work hard to make sure that our clients don't ever feel fleeced like that. Make sense?"

"Fleeced? Right, I know what you mean."

"Good. Also, I should say this: I guess our clients were tired of feeling frustrated that policies always seem to go up, while coverage always seems to go down. The big companies avoid paying any claims just at the time when you're suffering and need them the most. You tell me, what's worse than spending 45 minutes on hold when you're stuck by the side of the road in the rain?"

"Rain. Yes. Bad."

"Anyway, that's my rant. I get very stressed about bad service, don't you? Have you tried the quiche? It's quite lovely, isn't it?"

"Possibly. Err, no. Say, when can I come see you?"

"Well, I don't know. We'd have to block off at least 40 minutes for me to properly understand what's going on, what you need, and what's important to you. I don't suppose you're the kind of person that would invest that kind of time getting this kind of thing fixed once and for all, are you?"

"Sure, of course."

"I'm going to have lots of questions for you, you know, about your current policy and so on; and you'll probably have lots for me..."

That's how you get from "hello" to an up-front contract for a first exploratory meeting. It's how you go from being a salesperson to being a consultant—by asking questions.

If you sell insurance, start thinking about yourself as an insurance expert, a specialist with valuable knowledge and experience. You are well-trained and have a great pedigree. Your expertise is invaluable. You are a consultant. You are "Doctor Insurance."

If you are a real estate agent, start thinking about yourself as the realty expert, the realty consultant. "Doctor Realty."

If you are an [insert the industry that is relevant to your world], start thinking about yourself as the [insert industry] consultant.

THE DOCTOR'S OFFICE

Imagine walking into the doctor's office with a sore elbow. And imagine that, having made it into the exam room, you are greeted as follows:

"Ah, please take a seat."

"Thank you, Doctor."

"And, what might be the problem today?"

"It's my elbow, Doctor. It really hurts."

"Elbow, eh? Tricky things, elbows. I've never really been very good at elbows. How's your knee? I'm much better with knees."

"Um, no. It's my elbow."

"Right, right, of course, elbow, ha! Let me see." The doctor gets out a thick medical textbook, searches under "E" for elbow, and starts studying the diagram intently. "Is it bleeding?" he asks with his head still buried in the book. "Do you need to be administered oxygen, at all, do you think? Tell you what." He reaches for a tube of cream marked ACME Sore Elbow Cream. "Rub some of this cream on it three times a day. If it feels no better in a week, come back again for a closer look. Tell me, how's your family?"

I'm guessing that your level of confidence in Dr. Quack is pretty low right about now. If you're like me, you'd be heading for the door. Not exactly the consultant that you were hoping for. The doctor didn't seem knowledgeable, nurturing, caring, or expert. The doctor took no history; didn't even try to understand what the full picture was; and even prescribed without examining. All in all, the doctor seemed rather disinterested in your elbow's health and wellbeing. Not good.

How about this as an alternative consultative scenario?

"Ah, please take a seat."

"Thank you, Doctor."

"And, what might be the problem today?"

"It's my elbow, Doctor. It really hurts."

"Elbow, eh? Tricky things, elbows. I can see by the way that you're holding it that we're talking about your left elbow, correct?"

"Yes, it just started hurting last week."

"OK, so how about this? Let me start by asking you a few questions, getting a little history, and seeing if I can figure out what's going on. I'll then take a look at the elbow. I'll be as gentle as I can. I'll then maybe ask a few more questions, and we can take it from there. Is that fair?"

"Of course."

The doctor then asks one or more of the following questions, which is entirely consistent with the image and understanding of an expert in the field. With each question and answer, your confidence in the doctor grows and grows. Take a listen.

"When did the problem start?" [Always a good opening gambit.]

"Is it swollen?"

"Where up your arm does the pain start/stop?"

"Do your fingers tingle?"

"Is it a skin/irritation issue, a muscular issue, or a break, do you think?"

"Has this ever happened to you before?"

"Is it one elbow, or both?"

"Is it worse in the morning, in bed, in the evening?"

"Is it hot to the touch?"

"Does anything else seem amiss?"

"Are you taking any other medication at this time?"

"Did you bump or twist it in any way?"

"Do you play any sports?"

"Does anyone in your family have a similar issue?"

"Does it burn/throb/ache?"

"Is it sore to touch?"

...and so on, and so forth.

By the time the doctor orders an X-ray, suggests a cream, or puts your arm in a splint, you're wondering who else at the tennis club might benefit from this level of professionalism.

Why? Because the doctor asked about a million questions—questions that were: entirely pertinent; salient to the answers to prior questions; designed to gain a full understanding of the situation; intended to put the patient at ease; and demonstrating skill, knowledge, and experience. That's exactly what good consultants do. So, why don't salespeople as experts and consultants in their fields behave the same way? Those who do, succeed; those who don't, well, they continue to dance the dance to the tune that the piper plays.

Let's pretend that the second doctor orders a battery of tests—blood work, X-rays, an MRI, etc.—and calls you back for another consultation five days later.

"First of all," the doctor says, "you mustn't worry. I've looked at the tests and discussed them with a few colleagues I trust and who are experts in the field also. We've all come to the conclusion that you've got a clear case of [insert a reasonably painful, acute, common, and treatable elbow condition]. So, here's what we're going to recommend for treatment..."

How would you feel? You'd feel relieved. In fact, just talking to this doctor gives you and your elbow some sense of immediate comfort. The future looks better, and you will finally get to wear those high-tech tennis shoes you got for your birthday. You've found a professional who knows what to do, cares enough about you to do the job right, and has figured out a plan to make your situation better. It seems that the good doctor has become a trusted advisor (more on this later).

Suppose the doctor had said that although the professionals at the clinic had figured out exactly what was wrong with your elbow, it wasn't something that this particular doctor could help you with—but there was someone at the clinic who could. What's more, there was a spot on the calendar tomorrow for you to consult with that other doctor. How would that make you feel? Better. Would you feel any less grateful? No. Would you feel that your doctor was a charlatan to have the professional humility to say that your case needed attention from another expert? Would you complain to the medical board? No, of course not.

Sometimes the best advice—the advice people are willing to pay for—is not what they were hoping to hear. As human beings go (the smart ones, anyway), the folks who give that kind of advice are the ones people most respect.

CHAPTER SUMMARY

- Stop selling, start consulting. Ask a million pertinent questions.
- Ask questions; question answers.

> *"The one who asks questions does not lose his way."*
> —Akan proverb

CHAPTER 8

You Scratch My Back, I'll Scratch Yours

Stop being an unpaid consultant.

Start saying (and believing you have a right to say), "I'll do A for you, if you do B for me. Is that fair?"

If both propositions are reasonable and equitable, who could possibly disagree? If they aren't, shouldn't both parties discuss that up front?

In the previous chapter we talked about the significant benefits of adopting more of a consultative approach to your questioning. Remember, being a consultant is very good. Being an unpaid consultant, however, is very bad.

When prospects and customers ask you to do something (and they will), some of the requests will be fine, fair and natural; others will be so far over and above what any normal, sane observer not quite as mired in the process as yourself might consider bizarre.

Yet you somehow feel compelled to acquiesce, to capitulate, and to deliver.

This might be a simple but devastating request, like, "Drop the price," or it might be something more complicated like, "Change your processes/rules/procedures/whatever just for me." When the request appears, it's time to start asking more questions.

Your first inclination might not be to ask questions, though. It might be to try to figure out what has to be done in order to fulfill the request to the very best of your personal and business capability. You might sometimes justify the request by saying something soothing to yourself that sounds like, "Well, it's called customer service, or customer centricity, or putting the customer at the heart of everything we do," or some other such honorable and well-meaning customer philosophy.

Sometimes, this kind of thinking can stop you from saying what you really want to say but don't have the bravery (or the money in the bank) to say. Admit it: Deep down, in your heart of hearts, don't you want to say: "Not a chance! Who do you think you are? The gall!" But you don't.

When suspects/prospects/clients ask you to do something for them, you fight the urge to shout because you are caught up in the following overriding thoughts.

> You are eager to remain on the prospect's good side. What's more, you never want to give the prospect any reason to consider asking the same question of Rival Company, do you? Rival Company needs to be kept out of the picture at all costs.
>
> So, you do what you're told.
>
> You do genuinely want to help—you are, after all, the most responsive supplier in the industry. You pride yourself

on your super-high levels of customer service—it's in your vision statement, after all, which is printed on the back of your business card, remember?

So, you do what you're told.

When people in authority (clients and bosses) ask you to do something, you try your very best to do it. It makes your parents proud, of course—and everyone wants to keep their parents happy.

So, you do what you're told.

Prospects/clients demand, salespeople serve; it's just how the world is—even if the prospect doesn't need it. It's a power game that is set up to remind you of who's the boss around here.

So, you do what you're told.

Everyone knows how difficult it is to get a new customer. You've read the statistics that show how time serving existing customers is better spent than looking (prospecting) for new ones. This means that when you get clients, you go above and beyond to keep them.

So, you do what you're told.

You are so invested in the process and have spent so much time, effort, and energy pursuing the business, that one last thing—like shredding the profit margin out of existence—seems a relatively small price to pay.

So, you do as you're told.

You have made a promise to your sales manager that the project is in the bag and it's been on your prospect sheet and monthly reports for so long that to lose the deal now would be politically and financially embarrassing.

So, you do what you're told.

Let's face it. There are a million other good and reasonable reasons to do what you're told.

To be clear, I am not saying that it's time to get tougher with your clients just for the sake of getting tougher. But, as the old expression has it, "One hand washes the other." That's not a bad business philosophy, either, if you stop to think about it.

So let's start to use requests from prospects strategically. Let's commit to figuring out how important the requests really are, whose work you're being asked to do (and why), what's in it for you, and, last but certainly not least, whether agreeing to do them will drive you closer to or further from getting/keeping those orders. Is that fair? Of course, it's fair.

THE MOST IMPORTANT SINGLE QUESTION TO ASK

The single best opening gambit in almost every selling situation is obtaining the prospect's permission to ask lots of questions. It's very simple, very powerful, it works on both your and the buyer's attitude to each other, and it sounds like this:

"So, Omar, in order that I can really understand some of the issues you're facing and to try to see the world through your eyes, I'm going to be asking some specific and sometimes quite probing questions during our meeting. It will really help us figure out whether my company is the best fit for you at this stage. Does that make sense?"

Or like this, if you're a little more of a novice:

"So, Omar, I really want to try to understand what's going on in your world at the moment. Would you mind if I ask you some questions during the meeting?"

Either question is great, since either question unlocks a whole new world of equal business stature. It sets you up as much more of a consultant and gives you permission to ask (not simply answer) important questions.

If, after reading this entire book, you do no more than adopt this single strategy as your opening "let's get down to business" segue after talking about the weather and the price of fish, then your sales life will already be significantly changed for the better.

It's time to start instituting some reciprocity in the sales arena. Tell your prospects, in effect, "You scratch my back, I'll scratch yours." Fair's fair, after all. Sales is a two-way street, so let's start making this concept better heard. Let's first believe it, and then start saying it. But, as ever, there's the right way to say it—and the right way to say it is in a question, what else?

Let's take a look.

At some time or another, your prospect (or client) will likely ask you for something unusual (I say "unusual," but, let's be frank, these sorts of requests are not in the least bit unusual). Choose from any of the following typical examples:

- Better prices
- Another presentation
- Extended payment terms
- An annual stock cleanse
- Preferential delivery terms
- Increased credit
- Consignment stocking
- Dedicated hot line
- A face-to-face meeting with the CEO
- Tickets to the Super Bowl
- More of your time, effort, or attention than an account of that strategic significance deserves
- Free drawings/plans/proposal/machinery/equipment, etc.

- Discounted/replacement stock
- Cheaper/faster/wider delivery
- Free/discounted trials
- Staff training
- Or a million other similar requests

You get the picture.

You have a right to ask questions when this kind of request comes up. In order to exercise that right, though, you need to first decide whether you are a mouthpiece, a messenger, or a manager. Here's a quick description of each.

- **The Mouthpiece:** If your answer to client or prospect requests is to always quote the party line, company policy, and standard operating procedure, you're a mouthpiece. Nothing is as infuriating to prospects and customers as when they meet one of these political "we do things by the book" types. Take time to try to figure out why they're asking, at least.
- **The Messenger:** If you find yourself always saying, "I'll have to ask my boss," whenever you get asked anything more complex than, "How's your day?," what does that do to your status in the eyes of the customer/prospect? Even if it happens to be true and you do have to ask your boss, your first job is to figure out why this request, why now, what's going on, and what it's worth to you and your company to accede to the request.
- **The Manager:** Your first job, therefore, is to ascertain what's in it for you and the company and to explore alternative scenarios before taking the message back to headquarters. Your boss will appreciate the professionalism, and clients will learn that they don't have to go directly to your boss every time someone in Accounts (or Logistics, or IT, or wherever) sneezes.

How do you get this knowledge? By asking lots of smart questions. This has the added benefit of raising your status in the eyes of the client since you are becoming more consultative in your approach, as well as demonstrating to the client the extent, breadth, and depth of your knowledge and skill.

If you are where the buck stops and the decision is entirely yours, you also have to try to figure out what's going on and whether the request might be turned into a genuine win-win and on what and whose terms. Again, good questioning gets you to the truth and helps you to make the right, best decision.

As discussed earlier, let's not rely on the psychic skills of a local medium. Let's not get out the Ouija board to consult with the vapors; let's not try a Vulcan mind meld. Let's instead ask the client some really good pertinent and probing questions to get the needed understanding.

WHAT THE MANAGER'S QUESTIONS SOUND LIKE

To ask questions as a manager would, first figure out if the request is genuine. Sometimes your beloved and esteemed prospects ask you to do something that they know won't fly. They ask in an effort to trip you up, or get something that no one else could possibly give them, or waste your time chasing shadows, or frustrate you into backing out of the process, or use your agreement to beat up the other incumbent, and so on. This isn't a case of *caveat emptor*, it's a case of *caveat venditor* (let the seller beware).

To help you figure all this out, you can invite the prospect to play the "Let's Pretend" game. Take a listen.

Client Carlos says, "I'm hoping you can authorize a 15% discount. Possible?"

You say, "Carlos, that's a good question." [Stroke.] "Can I

authorize a 15% discount for your next order?" [Repeat/restate/rephrase.] "Hm, I don't know. Why do you ask?" [Reverse.]

"Well," he'll say, "it's in order to keep the people in Purchasing from going out to competitive tender." [Or some other such reason.]

"Right, a competitive tender. Do you think that's likely?"

"Oh sure. They were talking about it at the review meeting last week."

"Right, the review meeting. Makes sense. What do you think will happen if we can't swing that kind of discount for an order of this size?"

"We might have to farm it out to tender, like I said."

"Oh sure, tender, yes. Well fine, I think I can see that that's not going to be in anyone's interests, right?"

"Right."

"Who do you think you'd go to if it was going to be put on the open market?"

"Well, I don't know. Maybe the guys at Arden Hall Communications. You know how eager they are to get the business."

"Oh sure. The Arden Hall team is really good, I've heard good things about it. The company has a solid reputation and can always be seen in your market around here. Why didn't you go to them in the first place, anyway?"

"I wanted to use you guys. You know that you're my favorite supplier for this stuff."

"Thanks. Why though?"

"You always seem to deliver on time, and we get so few mistakes on the invoicing."

"Lovely. But I'm not sure we could go as deep as 15% on this one, Carlos. We always price fairly at around market rate, as you know. Say, let's pretend for a second, and I'm not saying that we could, but let's pretend [there's that phrase] that I could try hard to get you, maybe, a 4% rebate. Would that keep the Purchasing folks off your back this time, do you think?"

"Maybe."

"I wouldn't want to go pushing my head office for something that isn't going to fly. Can you find out for me, and let me know before I ask them? Does that make sense?"

"Sure, I guess."

"Thanks. Oh, and I'm not saying that we can or we can't, but let's pretend that we can. What would you do then?"

"I'd get the order over to you by this afternoon, for sure."

"Hm. That would be nice, but, hey, we can't win them all can we, Carlos? But, again, let's imagine that we can't go for the 4% either. Let's say that we can't give you anything at all in the way of discount. What else could we do to keep the business, do you think? Can you ask Purchasing that for me, too? In fact, shall I ask them for you? Would that help at all?"

"Hm, I'm not sure. Let me ask them. I'll get back to you."

"Right, right. So what about this as the next step? You ask Purchasing what a 4% rebate would do for us, as well as what other things we could do to keep the business if we can't cut deeply enough right now. Because, as you say, we always work hard on not letting you down, right?"

"Right."

"Great. Oh, one last thing, what do you think your customer, or even, God forbid, your boss would say if the order went to Arden Hall this time, and they somehow didn't quite deliver as well as we do?"

"I don't want to even think about that one!"

"Ha, I bet. Why? What do you think would happen if it somehow all went south?"

"I figure the brown lumpy stuff would hit the go-round air-making thing."

"Heads would roll."

"Right."

"Job losses in the warehouse?"

"For sure."

"Cancelled holidays to Acapulco, I'd bet too."

"Yeah, at the very least."

"Not fun."

"No."

Get the drift? Every single thing you as the seller said above ended in a question designed to steer Carlos to discover for himself that the best solution (the most peace-of-mind solution) would be for him to help you fight hard with Purchasing to keep the order with your name on the top of it. The "Let's Pretend" game (sometimes called the "If You Had a Magic Wand" game) is a powerful mechanism for helping flush out phantom or ill-conceived requests.

THE OTHER CONVERSATION

Above, we explored what the world might look like if you, the supplier, could or couldn't give Carlos the kind of discount he was seeking. But what do you get in return if you can give him the discount, other than the order that he's promised you? The order isn't enough, not by a long stretch, so let's get after something else. This is the bit that separates the wheat from the chaff. Let's pick up the thread after Carlos has spoken to Purchasing.

"So, Carlos, you're telling me now that unless I can drop 4%, the order will have to go to Arden Hall, is that it? Despite the risks that we talked about?"

"I'm afraid so."

"Well, OK, thanks for going into bat for me. Let me think about it. Other than the order, what else can you give me to go bargain with on your behalf when I go into bat for you?"

Do you see how the relationship, even in spite of the difficult negotiations, has taken very much of a partnership tone? It's you and the buyer against the rest of the world, including the Arden Hall gang. Remember, posture and questioning have got us there.

NINJA STATUS

Do you feel brave enough yet to say/ask something like this, I wonder?

"Carlos, I had a question just like that a few months ago, from another company—about the same size, and same product group that we are discussing here. The buyer asked me for a big discount, just like you. I went back to my boss and fought and fought like crazy for the buyer; he was a good guy, and I wanted to try to help, you know? Guess what? After three intense negotiations and four hours spent with our lead production guys and Purchasing, I managed to get 8% discount as a one-off. Then, guess what the buyer did? He showed our discounted quote to our competitors, and we lost the order. Not only did we lose the order (which was a disappointment, of course), but the real issue was that I lost the respect of my manager. I really can't have that happen again. Tell me, if I try to get a price reduction for you in this instance, and I'm not saying I can, what will you guys do?"

Emotional.

Bingo!

CHAPTER SUMMARY

- Are you a mouthpiece, a messenger, or a manager?
- To figure out what's real, play the "Let's Pretend" game.

> *"You cannot be fair to others without first being fair to yourself."*
> —Vera Nazarian

PART 3

Stop Hogging All the Airtime

In Part 2, we explored how important it is to interrupt the pattern and to be different from your competitors. Remember, you can't be better than your competitors if you are exactly like them. To be better, you have to first be different. Asking great questions, getting to the real truth, and creating equal business stature with the prospect are all critical differentiators. We also discussed how asking questions is the very best way to serve your prospects well because it's the very best way to understand them.

In Part 3, we will explore the best questioning techniques to employ and when to employ them. Finally we will help you by providing over 100 real-life strategic and tactical questions for you to start using right away in your quest for greater understanding and greater control of the sales process.

So, let's waste no time—let's keep going. There are new and bigger deals to be won.

CHAPTER 9

It's a Two-Way Street

A young, impressionable lad with an open and inquiring mind asks his loving father, "Dad, why is the grass green?"

"Good question, son. It's something to do with the sun, I think. Wait. It's chlorophyll. Or is it both? Hm, I'm afraid that I don't quite know. Sorry."

"Oh, OK. Well, why is the sky blue then?"

"Again, good question. It's the sun again, I think. No, wait, water vapor. Yes, water vapor. Hm. Maybe. No, sorry, pass."

"OK. Well, why do I have five fingers, not four, or six? Six would be much better, right?"

"Well... Nope. Drawing a blank again. No idea. Um, evolution, I guess? Opposable thumbs, yes, that's it. Flint hammers and axes, or something. Don't know, sorry."

"Daddy, do you actually mind me asking all these questions?"

"No, of course not, son. If you don't ask, how will you ever learn?"

The son stares at his father in deep puzzlement.

Very young children learn by asking questions about their world. First, they recognize a gap in their knowledge, and this engages their curiosity. Children are filled with wonder and natural curiosity, but as they grow older, they reach the point where they have a working knowledge of things around them. Then, for a whole stack of reasons, they simply stop asking questions.

The picture (the internal paradigm of rules and norms) that people create of their own reality serves to carry them through their daily lives reasonably unscathed. As long as the world presents itself in a non-threatening or unusual way and does not challenge belief systems, people can remain happy and content. They have enough information to go through the motions without having to think or question too much.

But then, some people start to struggle against their deep-seated biological and sociological programming by learning to ask questions again—smart questions, hopefully. These questions are smart enough for salespeople to encourage their prospects to see, understand, or believe the world to be different from the picture (paradigm) that they are carrying around in their own heads. For salespeople to be able to do this quickly and smoothly, naturally and conversationally, they must nurture a high level of healthy curiosity and possess an extremely high level of competence in questioning skills. In this chapter, you'll start moving toward mastery of this critical part of the salesperson's job.

Why do you need to be so skilled at asking questions? Consider the following exchange and ask yourself how often something like it happens when you first meet a new prospect.

> Hello, Salesperson from ABC Company. Thanks so much for coming to see me today. To help you properly qualify me and get the ball rolling, let me share with you a few basics.

Look, I have 30 minutes set aside in my calendar for this meeting, but I've made sure that we won't be interrupted. If we have to stretch to 45 minutes, that's OK with me. If we don't get to a good point by then, let's schedule to meet again on Friday morning.

I'm highly visual too, so try to keep your language consistent with how I like to see the world and process information.

I've never bought what you're selling before, so I am a little concerned about not knowing as much as I think I should; I have looked at some research and I see that you're very well regarded in the marketplace, so I expect to be in safe hands.

I've managed to secure $10,000 budget for this project—but that's my absolute ceiling.

My three major issues are A, B, and C; and I've had them for two years. I've tried x, y, and z to fix them, with little to no effect.

I calculate that these three issues have cost me about $100,000 over the last year alone, and my spouse tells me that if I don't get them fixed by the end of July, I'll be divorced by September.

Ask me anything you like, and I swear on my children's college funds that I will tell you the truth, the whole truth, and nothing but the truth.

Finally, I will have to run the proposal by my CFO, who's on holiday until Thursday. Let's at least agree to make a firm decision by the end of the week. How does that look to you? Fair enough?

How often do prospects do that? Not very often—that's how often. In fact, let me amend that: Never! They never do that, period.

To make matters worse, when prospects do start talking, they will likely mislead you by telling you a special version of the truth designed, in their view, to protect themselves or elicit the kind of response from you that they most want to hear/believe. Or both.

None of that helps you, the seller, qualify or disqualify the prospect. As we have seen, this leads to masses of time, money, effort, and energy being wasted on prospects who are not qualified to purchase from you.

Then, as if to add further insult to injury, when your prospects do ask you a question, you (the salesperson) may just answer it as honestly, as diligently, and as accurately as possible. Sure, that makes the Parent voice in your head happy by reminding you what a good and clever person you are for answering the nice prospect's questions as truthfully as possible—but you are over all of that nonsense by now, aren't you? Good.

Sales can be a rather nasty business at times.

Let's imagine that a prospect asks Alice, a salesperson, "Alice, how many offices do you have?"

Let's imagine that the company that Alice works for has one office. Should Alice simply say, "We have just one office"? No, no she shouldn't!

First, before Alice answers anything, she needs to try to figure out why the prospect is asking that particular question, in that particular way, at this particular time, and why it might be important to the prospect to know how many offices Alice's company operates.

Take a minute or two to try figure out what could be behind the prospect's question. Try to imagine at least five reasons why

Alice's prospect might be asking about the number of offices she has. Think about these possible motives that the prospect might have for asking the question.

The prospect could be thinking:

- "I want to work with a company that is large enough to manage my important business."
- "I want to work with a company that has offices in New York, as well as California," where the prospect also has a second office.
- "I want to work with a small company where I would be a very big fish in their very small pond."
- "I equate 'many offices' with 'longevity' and 'permanence,' which are important to me."
- "I think lots of offices means high overhead, which means high prices for smaller customers like me."
- "I think lots of offices means lots of support staff and lots of expertise to help me out if I ever have a problem."
- "I want to deal with a salesperson on a small team, and lots of offices will mean lots of junior salespeople looking after my account."
- "I'm just curious."
- "I'm just making conversation."

The key word to all of the above is "could." Alice doesn't know what the prospect is thinking, but it could be anything.

To make things even more confusing and bewildering, Alice is likely to overlay her own belief systems onto why the prospect has asked the question in the first place. Nightmare!

If you (the salesperson) believe that having only one office says something unflattering about you or your company, you may try to dodge the question or answer it in a vague manner. Before you realize it, you are sounding like every other run-of-the-mill, slightly crooked salesperson the world over. Drat!

On the other hand, if you believe that having a single office is somehow a good thing, you shout about the fact in the belief that the prospect feels exactly the same way that you do. Guess what? The prospect almost certainly doesn't. However, since people are programmed to answer questions, you either say that you have one office with pride or you wince when you declare the paltry number and hope for the best. Or worse, you dodge the question entirely, leaving the prospect wondering why you're being slippery and what else you might try to hide later. Double drat!

Consider how many vastly different interpretations could attach to any of these questions:

- "How many offices do you have?"
- "How long have you been in business?"
- "How similar is your business to your biggest competitor?"
- "Can we have better purchasing terms?"
- "If I give you this business, how often will I see you?"

There are literally hundreds of ways to answer such questions, and there are thousands of possible intentions lying at the heart of these questions. Guess what? The real answer lies in the prospect's head, not yours.

To put it another way, what comes out of the prospect's mouth is rarely if ever what goes into the salesperson's ears.

Look at that last question again, that "How often will I see you?" query. It's a really tricky one.

The answer almost certainly isn't, "As many times as you need to see me." If that's the answer you give, be prepared to ask the hotel nearest the customer if you can rent a room there 11 months per year.

Nor is the correct answer, "Clients with revenues at your level can expect to receive what we call our 'Premium' status. This means that I will see you every two days without fail." That's what prospects want to hear. Don't say it.

The point is, you cannot successfully answer any question without first understanding what's at the heart of the question from the client's perspective. What is the real motivation behind the question?

Consider the table below. All of the interpretations made by this lackluster salesperson sound plausible, don't they?

When the prospect asks…	The salesperson might think…
Can you get me the quotation out by Friday?	I must try to get the quotation out by Friday, so I'll clear my calendar.
Can I bring our CFO to the meeting next week?	Yay, he's bringing the CFO. He must be really serious about our proposal—this one's practically in the bag.
Will you send some literature over?	He's really interested—he wants to see our literature, goody!
Can I take a few days to think about it?	He's really interested—he wants to think about it! Great.
Are you able to ship on Euro Pallets?	If we can ship on Euro Pallets we might get the job; if we can't we almost probably won't. I'll ask the CEO to order some Euro Pallets right away.
Why don't you go ahead and set us up on your purchasing system?	The order is mere days away, for sure. I'll advise the factory manager to ramp-up production.

When was your company founded?	He's concerned that we're only three years old. Before I answer him, I will explain to him how we handle some of the largest accounts in the state, and that we manage to process over 30 orders a week, and that we just bought a brand new packaging line to automate all shipments to Brazil, and that both of our founders went to the same university as him and that we had an article in the newspaper praising us for being one of the fastest growing businesses in our sector.
Do you sell to Big Box Store?	Big Box Store is our biggest customer, and we are very proud of that, so I will, of course tell him that we do—I'm so glad that he asked me that one.
Can you tell me more about the warranty period?	Oh no, I was dreading this issue coming up; our warranty isn't nearly as good as our competitor's. I'll offer him a 10% reduction straight away and see if that placates him.

Every single assumption above is all too likely to be wrong.

The correct response to practically all questions that might come your way during your life is to figure out why the prospect (or client, or spouse, or friend, or child) asked the question in the first place. Always think of questioning as a two-way street. Figure out what's really at the root of the question; then (and only then), answer the real question in a helpful manner. At Sandler, we call the art of answering a question with another question—in an attempt to get to the root issue—reversing. It takes practice. I'll show you how to do it in the next chapter.

CHAPTER SUMMARY

- Questioning is a two-way street. Not only should you ask your prospects/clients lots of questions, you should also ask them questions about the questions they ask you.
- You need to ask questions in order to get to the truth.

> *"It is not the answer that enlightens, but the question."*
> —Découverts

CHAPTER 10

How to Answer Questions with More Questions

Thus far, we've shown that giving good (accurate, complete, technically competent, clever, thorough, informed) answers to prospects'/clients' questions may feel, in the short term, like it gets a salesperson's own needs met, but in fact it significantly works against the salesperson. Sure, it may make the salesperson feel clever and special in the moment (it delights the Parent voices inside), but it has the opposite impact in the longer term.

This brings us to an important issue: How should a salesperson react when a question is asked?*

- Answer it?   No.
- Ignore it?   No.
- Mislead?   No.

---

* I'm talking about a significant question that affects your business relationship, of course, not questions like, "How are you today?," or, "Did you see the game last night?"

I do hope that by this point the right answer is second nature to you:

- You reply with another question.

Adherents of the Sandler Selling System start by learning a few basic questioning strategies and responses in their initial Sandler Foundations training. These question classifications are designed specifically to help sales professionals dig beneath the prospect's question in order to establish what's really going on: what's really being asked and why.

Let's take a look at these question types in their very simplest form. A little later on in the book, we will move on to more sophisticated questioning techniques designed to drive the prospect further down the road to truth.

THE MOMENT OF TRUTH

Let's imagine that you work for a logistics company that ships across the United States. You're with the buyer of a local manufacturer on the lookout for a new logistics supplier. You're about 20 minutes into the sales interview, when your prospect asks you a fairly innocuous question:

"So, tell me. Do you ship overnight to Richmond, and can you collect directly from the dockside at Baltimore harbor?"

Let's imagine that you can in fact do both of these things. In fact, let's imagine that you do it often and with some skill. Great! This is exactly the kind of question that you hope for all day. Perfect.

Scenario 1: Answer It

"Why, yes, yes we can. We run to Richmond daily, and we collect from Baltimore every other day!"

Beaming smile from you.
Big pat on the back for clever ol' you.
Cookie anyone?
Good answer?
No! It's entirely the wrong, completely wrong, definitely 100% wrong answer.

It's a terrible answer because it dead-ends the entire conversation.

By answering the question (albeit 100% truthfully), you did not learn anything. Why did the prospect ask that specific question? Why ask it now—specifically? What's going on—specifically? What has happened in the past—specifically?

By answering the question as it was presented, nothing new is learned by the salesperson.

NOTE: An infinitely worse answer would be to say something like this: "Why, yes! Yes, we can. We run to Richmond daily, and we collect from Baltimore harbor every other day. We've just taken delivery of three of the latest state-of-the-art Volvo FH Series trucks, and our brand-new computer software system was developed by NASA, and was commissioned by Bill Gates himself. Our latest award-winning warehouse has a chocolate river running through it based on Willy Wonka's chocolate factory, and all of the Oompa Loompas pack our crates…"

Resist the temptation to show off. It can only hurt you.

- What if the prospect thinks having a state-of-the-art facility means you're making too much money? Maybe you're overcharging?
- What if the prospect thinks you're being just a little too clever?
- What if the prospect thinks you're trying to close right now? No one likes that feeling.

- What if the prospect thinks you're showing off? (Which you are.)
- What if the prospect doesn't want to be a very small fish in your very big pond?
- What if [insert a million, billion other things the prospect might think that can hurt you]?

Don't answer, don't ignore, don't mislead—ask!

Scenario 2: Answer with a Question

The correct Sandler response to the prospect's question could take the form of any one of the following basic approaches.

The Reverse

"I'm glad you asked me that. Do we expedite to Richmond, and can we collect directly from the dock at Baltimore? Of all the questions you could have asked me, tell me, why are these particular two things important to you right now?"

Easy right? Super doable? It could easily become a habit. Do you see the difference? If not, put the book down and go have a nap. But if you're still with me, and I assume you are, read on. You are going to love these variations too.

The Negative Reverse

"Good question: Do we regularly haul to Richmond, and can we collect directly from the Baltimore dock? I don't suppose you'd want to share with me why those two things are important to you at this moment, would you?"

Nice. Gentle, supportive, subtle, interesting, warm, unpressured—like a brand new pair of fluffy slippers.

NOTE: You can usually tell when you're in negative-reverse-land. If your question starts with the words, "I don't suppose...," you're there. Basically, you position the question negatively by declaring up front that you don't expect the other person to answer, help, step in, or save you. Human beings like to help out the most when it is not assumed that they will. Negative reverses are an extremely powerful questioning technique and should be used often.

The Start-Stop Reverse

"Glad you asked me that. In actual fact, we do collect every day from…wait, hold on a second. Tell me, why do you ask?"

Lovely. It feels and sounds natural; it gets the prospect talking, not you, and you learn something new. Marvelous.

The Strip-Line Reverse

"Everyone seems to be asking me that these days—Baltimore to Richmond overnight. What is it about Baltimore to Richmond that everyone's so excited about?"

Bang! You stop talking. The prospect gets to explain what's so exciting. The prospect hears himself telling you what's the real story behind the question.

NOTE: If you're a keen angler, you'll be familiar with strip-lining; it's the practice of letting the fish take the bait and, instead of yanking on the line too quickly and risk the fish getting free, you let it swim off with the hook allowing it to become fully engaged. That way, when you do eventually tug on the line, the hook becomes deeply embedded, and it's curtains for poor ol' Moby Dick.

The Presumptive-Question Reverse

"We get asked that a lot: Do we ship to Richmond overnight, and can we collect from the harbor? I'm guessing that you are asking me specifically because most of your customers are in Richmond and most of your freight comes into the States in Baltimore. Is that about right, or am I missing something?"

Boom! You stop talking. The prospect either validates your version of reality or gives you a better explanation.

The Most-Important Reverse

"That's a super two-part question: Baltimore to Richmond, and overnight. I imagine that both elements are pretty important, but let me ask you this. Which is most important of the two, and why?"

Go to the head of the class!

The Multiple-Choice Reverse

"That's a great question: Do we overnight to Richmond, and can we collect from dockside? I usually get asked these types of questions when there's maybe a penalty for late deliveries, or when the customer doesn't want to even touch the product because he doesn't have adequate storage facilities, or maybe when the ultimate customer is in a rush—are any of these the case here?"

The prospect has the option of picking one of your good explanations, or offering another one. You shoot—you score!

The Dummy-Up Reverse

"Can we ship to Richmond, and can we collect directly from Baltimore? OK, I wasn't quite expecting that question. I'm not sure, but I'd be happy to go check. Why'd you ask? Is it really important to you that we maybe can?"

In this reverse, you pretend to know somewhat less about all this than you actually do. No problem—as long as it improves the informational quality of the conversation. Yes, I know that you are entirely sure that you can do exactly what the prospect is asking for, but just try to act a bit dumb for me for a minute and see what happens. The prospect gets to put on the know-it-all hat and starts opening up to you. It all works for your own good.

The Rule-of-Three Reverse

"So, great question: from Baltimore to Richmond overnight. You know when I get asked something like that, it's usually for one of three reasons. Either: 1) we have to haul really perishable cargo, and speed is the top, top priority, 2) you've maybe had problems in the past collecting from dockside in Baltimore, or 3) you have to send out of Richmond first thing in the morning for a further delivery, maybe through the airport over there. Am I on the right track, or have I completely missed the mark?"

Genius!

The Let's-Pretend Reverse

"Nice question: Baltimore to Richmond overnight. OK, let's pretend for a second that we could do those things. I'm not saying we can, but what might that mean to you if we could or couldn't?"

Brilliant!

The Off-the-Record Reverse

"What an interesting question. Look, off the record, which of these two concerns you most right now: Baltimore or Richmond?"

Lovely. Remember to reward yourself with a celebratory crumpet and a nice steaming hot mug of tea as soon as you get home.

The Competitive-Edge Reverse

"That's such a super question. Before I answer it, tell me, are these two things—Baltimore collections and overnight to Richmond—key to your own competitive edge at the moment? I'm guessing you asked for a reason—if so, why?"

The prospect cannot answer this without thinking. Thinking is good.

The Key-Strategy Reverse

"That's a great question, and I guess it's important to ship to Richmond overnight and collect from Baltimore too. Why are those two specific things tied to your key business strategy going forward?"

Smashing.

Summary of the Reverse Strategy

Why are these questions (reverses) so much better than puffing out your chest and saying, "Yes, yes we do! We are the local Baltimore and Richmond overnight shipping experts; ask anyone"?

It's because that sort of answer offers you no more knowledge or understanding. The information exchange is one-way. You don't discover why the prospect asked the question in the first place. In fact, you learn nothing by simply waiting to answer more questions—no matter how clever or accurate your answers may be.

Imagine that the buyer in Scenario 1 says, "OK then." After you have answered the question just as asked, where would that leave you? Nowhere, that's where! You've just been dead-ended.

The buyer cannot respond, "OK then," to any of your Scenario 2 responses. The prospect has to divulge something more—the conversation and the exchange must continue along a more informative path—and this is infinitely better for you.

Notice the framework of all of the Scenario 2 responses: stroke; repeat; reverse. This is one of the Sandler salesperson's most basic questioning/discovery techniques.

1. ***Stroke***—Most people didn't get enough hugs as babies, after all. Make prospects feel good about themselves—a very positive and developmental OK-ness approach.
2. ***Repeat***—Rephrase/restate. Prospects recognize that you're listening and understanding them.

3. ***Reverse***—Find out why the prospects are asking what they're asking. Answering the question at face value does not get you to the truth.

We call this sequence "SRR" for short. Now here's a question: How many times during a sales interview should you SRR or ask another question in response to a question asked of you? Let me answer that by asking you a question of my own. (Clever.) If I told you that the prospect/client should be talking at least 70% of the entire sales conversation, how many times would you think you need to SRR? Yes—that many. Gulp. You'd better put on your biggest and best practicing pants.

HOMEWORK

Write down a list of the 20 most common questions/statements/objections that you run into in your average work week. If you can't think of 20 right now, over the next month, every time a prospect, client, work colleague, or manager asks you a question, write it down. Then:

- Write down the question/statement/objection/demand.
- Write down what the person might be really asking/saying.
- Write down a good (conversational/nurturing) reverse question that helps you get to a hidden truth below the surface of the question—the question that helps you get to the reason that particular question was asked, and why now.

When the person gives you that answer, figure out what question to ask next. Keep the question types rotating so that you don't sound like some sort of manic parrot. It might look something like:

Prospect: Question
You: Stroke, reverse question
Prospect: Statement
You: Strip-line question
Prospect: Question
You: Stroke. Restate, rule-of-three question
Prospect: Statement
You: Presumptive question
Prospect: Statement
You: Stroke, repeat, reverse

Without wanting to suggest in any way that the buyer-seller interaction is the least bit aggressive, confrontational, or acrimonious, let me ask you to think of yourself as a boxer, sparring in the center of the ring with the prospect. You wouldn't simply stand still in the middle of the ring and jab, jab, jab, jab, jab, would you? If you did, you'd be back in the dressing room feeling rather sorry for yourself and reaching for the headache tablets pretty quickly. No, you'd move forward, you'd press, jab, fall back, upper cut, duck, roundhouse, one-two, dodge, weave, jab, cross, uppercut, counter, crouch, duck, cross, hook, and so on. You'd mix it up. You'd vary speed, rhythm, tempo, punches, and movement.

Well, your questioning strategy should be exactly the same. Mix it up, don't always do the same thing, and don't always be mechanical or predictable; otherwise, the next thing you'll be looking at is the ceiling, and the next voice you hear will be the referee shouting, "...9...and 10, you're out!"

CHAPTER SUMMARY

- Factual responses to the prospect's question—very bad!
- Varied questioning responses—very good!
- Stroke. Repeat. Reverse.
- Mix it up.

> *"Knowing the answers will help you in school. Knowing how to question will help you in life."* —Warren Berger

CHAPTER 11

From Knowing to Owning

> *The absent-minded maestro was racing up New York's Seventh Avenue to a rehearsal, when a stranger stopped him. "Pardon me," he said, "can you tell me how to get to Carnegie Hall?" "Yes," answered the maestro breathlessly. "Practice!"*
>
> **— E.E. KENYON, "THE WIT PARADE," 1955**

I know that the joke above is rather cheesy, but in Sandler, we talk a lot about transitioning from knowing to owning. Like most worthwhile pursuits, the journey requires the application of both persistence and practice. Dogged persistence and determined effort help you transition from simple knowledge-based remembering all the way to actual, on-the-job thinking—mental processing—in the most appropriate way. This skills journey is broken down into these stages, with only the last equating to what we call "owning."

- Awareness
- Knowledge
- Application
- Skills
- Habits

A shorthand way of looking at this that will save you having to memorize the list: AKASH.

You need to be sufficiently skilled in asking questions such that it is completely natural for you to elect to ask exactly the right question, at exactly the right time, in exactly the right way, to elicit exactly the right kind of response (thinking) from the prospect. In the heat of the battle, it really won't work for you to get your ready-reckoner and slide-rule out to try to figure out the best question to ask the prospect. It has to become as natural as breathing—it has to become habitual. If you're like most people, and the odds are pretty good that you are, you don't spend much of your day thinking about whether or not it's a good idea to breathe. You just do it. It's something over which you have, as the academics put it, unconscious competence.

This chapter is all about getting you to a position of unconscious competence.

This level of skill requires a significant understanding of the human condition, as well as a deep appreciation of the dynamics at play in human interaction and a solid grasp on the various factors that motivate human beings to think, believe, and act in specific ways. That sounds tricky, I know, but believe it or not, it all boils down to three simple steps.

- Step 1: Have a plan.
- Step 2: Have a sales system that allows you to control the buying/selling process.

- Step 3: Get permission to ask the right questions.

Yes, I know that last one sounds like it covers a whole lot of real estate. By "right questions," I mean questions that allow the prospects to discover a few basic things for themselves, namely:

- You are different from your competitors.
- You are better than your competitors.
- Prospects have a compelling need for you and your products and services (or, if they don't, you want them to realize that fact very quickly).*
- The best ultimate purchase decision is based not on price, but on value.

The right questions at the right time, in the right manner, for the right reasons, ensure that all of the above is achieved.

PRACTICE WITH DETERMINATION AND PURPOSE

Remember when you were first learning to drive? The very first time you sat behind the wheel probably felt pretty terrifying, I expect. Exhilarating, of course, but I am sure, like me, you were filled with trepidation. Unnerving, nail-biting stuff. Yet you didn't allow yourself to succumb to your fears and simply give up. Why?

I'm quite sure you don't remember trying to walk—you were only 12 months or so old at the time, after all. It must have seemed a difficult skill to master. If you've ever seen a child trying to stand for the first time and then to walk, it is a feat of almost superhuman effort and unwavering determination—despite falling down again and again and again. Despite the effort, children never give up. Why?

---

* Because if it's going to be a *no,* when do you want to know? That's right, now!

Likewise, remember learning to talk? That was tough.
What about learning to read? Ouch.
Writing? That took effort—a lot of it.
Using a fork? Hard.
Riding a bike? Impossible.
Learning to skate—swim—play the piano? Don't remind me.

Some things you just have to do, and no amount of failed attempts, painful bumps, or bruises (physical or mental) will stand in your way.

People are extremely determined critters when they want to be. How do I know? Everyone drives, walks, talks, reads, uses a fork, and so on, every single day.

When you first learned to drive, your mind was filled with rules, regulations, and unfamiliar sequences that simply had to be applied in one way, not another. Despite how unnatural they might have felt or the volume of your protest, you still simply had to drive one way (the way determined by the particular testing agency in your area) and not another (the way that you would perhaps have preferred to drive). The problem is, the internal combustion engine runs one way, not another; traffic signals work one way, not another; roads run one way, not another; speed limits are one way, not another.

In short, there are some things that work one way, not another. When people are determined to comply with the rules and regulations and put in the effort (despite how difficult it might be), they learn how to do it right.

Sales is exactly the same. Regardless of how difficult things may seem, the only way to get better at it is to practice, practice, practice until the process is natural and you don't have to think about it. If your goal is to reach the point where executing the skill is as normal as normal can be—the point of unconscious competence—you have to practice.

No matter how unnatural, uncomfortable, unfortunate, or plain downright difficult all of this may appear, the reality is this: It is time to practice because nothing trumps practice, practice, and then more practice (10,000 hours according to some). So, get going. The best time to start? Right now—time's a wastin', so off you trot.

SOME QUESTIONS ARE MORE USEFUL THAN OTHERS

Is this a question?

Well, yes, of course it is—it ends with a question mark, after all.

But does it add to our understanding of anything about the prospect? No, not really. Is it a useful sales question, therefore? I would say not.

Swamis, gurus, and philosophers the world over like to ask enigmatic and impossible questions like:

- Can you step into the same river twice?
- If a tree falls in a forest and there's no one around, does it make a noise?
- What is the sound of one hand clapping?
- How do you know which armrest at the cinema is yours?

Tricky.

None of these are useful questions (not for our purposes, anyway).

Notice that, in the context of a sales conversation, some questions are more useful than others. Asking questions for the sake of asking questions is not what we have been talking about in this book. Moral: Don't turn into the "Why?" guy.

- You customer makes a statement, and you reply, "Why?"
- He replies to that, and you bark back, "Why?" again, and so on and so on.

That is not questioning. That is you being an idiot.

You're not learning anything new by being the "Why?" guy: you're not being clever, and you're not helping to facilitate any understanding at all—other than perhaps to illustrate why you are making no sales commissions.

Nor should you ask inappropriate questions—oblique non sequiturs—questions that are not asked to further the conversation and its related discovery down a particular avenue of understanding. This line of questioning, for instance, is right out:

Prospect: How are you today? It's been a while.

Salesperson: Did you see the game last night?

Prospect: Uh, no, I didn't. Are you well? You look well.

Salesperson: Do you prefer strawberry ice cream to chocolate? I like chocolate, mostly.

Prospect: Uh...

Salesperson: Have you ever wondered how they get the non-stick stuff to stick to the frying pan?

Prospect: ...?...

Salesperson: Is that your coat? I like coats. Do you like coats? Coats are brilliant.

Prospect: Security!

QUESTIONING WITH SKILL

There are a wide variety of questioning strategies the world over, but you could do worse than adopting the approach taken by Socrates nearly 2,500 years ago—anything that has endured that long might have something to teach us.

The Socratic questioning method proposes six basic types of questions. Let's take a look at how one might apply these Socratic principles to the task of posing questions during a discussion with a prospect.

1. *Questions for clarification*
   - Why do you say that?
   - How does this relate to our discussion?
   - What do you mean by that?
   - Which means…?

2. *Questions that probe assumptions*
   - What could we assume instead?
   - How could we verify [x]?
   - What do you think would happen if…?
   - You seem to be assuming [x]. Am I right?

3. *Questions that probe reasons and evidence*
   - Can you give me an example of that?
   - What do you think has caused that to happen, and why?
   - Were the results what you expected?
   - How often does this affect you in this way?

4. *Questions about viewpoints and perspectives*
   - What would be an alternative way to get this done?
   - What is another way to look at it?
   - Can you explain why [x] is necessary or beneficial, and who benefits?
   - What are the strengths and weaknesses of…?

5. *Questions that probe implications and consequences*
   - What generalizations can you make about [x]?
   - What are the consequences of that assumption?
   - What are you implying?
   - How does [x] tie in with what we learned before?

6. *Questions about the question*
   - Then what would happen?
   - Why do you think I asked you that?
   - Of all the questions to ask me, why that one?
   - Which of your questions means the most to you?

HOMEWORK

Write down the questions you get asked on a daily/weekly basis. Before too long, you'll start to identify some trends. Group the questions together, and identify the top 20 questions you get asked more than any other.

Some of these questions will be more difficult to answer than others, and some of them (perhaps because they feel easy and straightforward) you might answer too readily without investigating further. For each of these top 20 questions, write down an appropriate Socratic reverse—and not just for the purposes of clarification. Craft reverses that really probe what's going on, what's behind the intention of the question.

Start to try to use these probing reverses out in real sales situation—again, and again, and again—until they become second nature. Before too long (it may take a couple of months, but you're determined), you'll find they feel as natural as walking.

Once you have these types of questions at your fingertips, once they trip appropriately and readily from your tongue with conviction, once you can mix-and-match them with skill and ease, you will have arrived at a state of unconscious competence—just like you have for driving/walking/talking/reading, remember? This is where the fun begins (and the sales start to roll in).

By the same token, once you know the Sandler selling process in great detail, can pass up and down the submarine easily (without thinking), and have a ready and appropriate question right at hand, you will have started to own, not simply know, the system. That takes practice, dear reader. You have to start practicing. Today.

CHAPTER SUMMARY

- Getting to a level of unconscious sales competence requires a little professional humility, a lot of practice, and a lot of determined application.
- Understand what you want to know, and then ask the right question to give you that answer.

> *"If you do not ask the right questions, you do not get the right answers."*
> —Edward Hodnett

CHAPTER 12

Qualify, Qualify, Qualify

When you qualify hard, the close is easy. When you qualify too easily, the sale is almost impossible.

Remember in Chapter 2 when we examined a typical buyer-seller interaction? Remember the challenges with which the traditional seller is presented when, at the end of the sales process (which is controlled by the buyer), the seller finds himself in chase mode and voicemail jail? Remember how the buyer languishes in the safety and anonymity of the buyer's Witness Protection Program?

Did you ever wonder why all that happens?

One of the big reasons for this sorry state of affairs is that the sellers do not properly qualify their prospects. They are too keen to chase the pot of gold at the end of the mythical sales rainbow. Or rather, they thought they were qualifying, but in fact they were engaged in some other activity. A qualification process that is too inclusive, too easy, or too gentle makes the finish line—the close—too difficult. A natural consequence of this frenzied activity, otherwise known as constantly running toward anyone with a pulse, is lots of travelling to lots of meetings, talking to lots of people, churning out lots of quotations, while achieving very low conversions rates.

But, being busy is a good thing, right? No, actually.

Most salespeople, when complaining about their situation, report that time is their biggest enemy. There are lots of quotations to prepare, lots of critical sales to close, lots of meetings to have, with lots of important people. Normally, when the sales manager asks about the upcoming week, salespeople quickly morph into the much-beleaguered White Rabbit from Disney's *Alice in Wonderland*, eloquently declaring, "I'm late! I'm late! For a very important date! No time to say hello, goodbye! I'm late! I'm late! I'm late!"

Letting your boss see the pile of paperwork, the busy desk, the late-into-the-night emails, the endless hotel receipts, the long list of telephone messages, and the frantic beads of sweat on your terribly furrowed brow can't hurt your job security. Who else could possibly absorb this level of detail and complexity if, God forbid, you were to go under a bus tomorrow—or, worse, get offered a job by your competitor? It's heavily in salespeople's interests to give off the clear message that the business would simply collapse without them on the team. "Just look at the number of quotations that I do every month!"

It's reassuring to feel busy, valuable, and indispensable, isn't it?

What's more, most sales managers give their salespeople hard targets based on: number of quotations per month; total value quoted; number of presentations delivered, and so on. Then, they penalize those salespeople who do not consistently tick the correct boxes on their monthly sales reports. These sales managers tend to adopt a spaghetti-sales approach to business: Throw enough sales activity at the wall, and eventually something is bound to stick. Most salespeople, therefore, are trained to demonstrate business "busyness" rather than sales skill.

Busy can be seen by all—it looks like lots of ticks on the weekly sales activity sheet. Busy is good. Busy is rewarded.

How many times do average sales managers, when trying to improve the skills of average (yet very busy) salespeople after the compulsory annual performance review, simply send the salespeople to a time-management course?

Poor time management is not the main issue. It's poor prospect management, client management, territory management, or self-image management. Look to these for the real issue.

WHAT THE BEST SALESPEOPLE DO

The very best salespeople the world over spend much more time than everybody else prospecting and properly qualifying their live prospects and client opportunities and much less time than everybody else quoting, presenting, and trying to close business they have no chance of winning. Even though absolute numbers of quotations (and checks on a pointless sales activity report) may seem low, the conversion rates and the average order value dramatically climb. Customer churn rates and average sales cycles dramatically drop, too.

This is called a win-win. This is good.

How do they pull it off? They actually use questions to disqualify potential buyers. They go for the *no*. Can you imagine?

One of the most counterintuitive approaches that Sandler acolytes espouse is that of gently but insistently pushing unqualified prospects away. Most salespeople seem to spend their lives encouraging prospects to move toward them, to move toward the sales "light." "Cross over, children. All are welcome. There is peace and serenity in the Light." They have a "come closer to me, salvation lies with me" approach to sales development.

But Sandler salespeople take the entirely opposite approach—180 degrees the other way. Sandler-trained sales managers realize that it's a perfectly good thing (and should be actively encouraged) to visit with fewer prospects, create fewer quotations, deliver fewer proposals, and spin fewer, but better qualified, plates.

The broad principle is this: Start to push prospects away (gently, firmly, and with a nurturing voice). If they resist, if they push back, if they insist on continuing the conversation, then they are entirely serious in their interest in you; if they go away, they never were.

Not only does this "arm's length" approach to the sale go a long way to keeping the balance of power much more equal between the buyer and the seller, it also saves the harried salesperson an awful lot of time, effort, and energy—time, effort, and energy that would be better spent prospecting rather than quoting business for the sake of ticking a box and keeping the sales manager happy.

"How," you ask, "do we keep pushing prospects away? How do we test their mettle, their resolve, their genuine interest in us?" Well, by asking questions, of course.

You must accept, though, that questions for their own sake are not enough. You have to think about what is meant by the answers. You can't be too keen to hear what you want to hear—you don't want to have "happy ears." That's what happens when you read between the lines and insert what you hope the prospect is saying/asking. You don't want to become addicted to "hopium."

You want to ask enough questions to verify that what you think the other person said is what was actually said—and intended. That's essential to qualifying.

Let's take a look at a few examples. As you read the questions that follow, see if you can pick up on the principles of:

Equal business stature between buyer and seller.

Adopting a nurturing sales tonality.

Making sure you understand properly before you respond.

Not being too keen to proceed.

Your time is valuable, too, and you're not a pushover. You're curious, skeptical, and not too attached to the outcome, remember?

Add it all up, say it in your best, most helpful Nurturing Parent voice, and suddenly you're in a conversation that doesn't sound like a conversation with a salesperson.

Prospect Translation Guide		
When prospects say…	**…they might actually be saying…**	**To verify, ask something like…**
"Hmm, that sounds interesting. Can you send me a brochure, and call me back next week?"	"I don't have time for this right now, but I don't want to appear rude, so I'll just say this to get you off the phone."	"I'd be glad to do that, but let me ask you this: Sometimes when I hear, 'Send me a brochure,' what I'm actually hearing is that the person is not really interested and is trying to get rid of me. Is that what's really going on here? You can tell me, I'm a grown-up."

Prospect Translation Guide

When prospects say…	…they might actually be saying…	To verify, ask something like…
"Sure, call me back next Friday afternoon."	"Let me escape for now. I'll deal with maybe ducking the call on Friday. I'm not in on Friday anyway. This gives me time to think about it without feeling rushed by a salesperson."	"I'll put you in my calendar for Friday at 3:00. Tell me, what should I do if I can't get hold of you on Friday at 3:00?"
"Let me think about it."	"No, thanks."	"Is that your way of saying, 'No thanks, this time around'? Can we agree to make a decision now, and if it's a *no*, that's perfectly OK?"
"I'll have to ask my manager. Call me next week; we'll let you know."	"I have to ask my manager." …or… "No." …or… "I need to think about it."	"Of course, that makes perfect sense. Tell me, if she asks you for your opinion on the matter, what will you say to her? What do you think she'll say about that? Look, would it make sense for me to talk to her, too?"
"Your price seems a little high."	"It's my job to say that you're a little too high, even if you're not."	"Well, no surprise, we're rarely the cheapest, after all. 'A little high' in this instance means what exactly?"

Qualify, Qualify, Qualify

Prospect Translation Guide		
When prospects say...	**...they might actually be saying...**	**To verify, ask something like...**
"We have a competitive bid process, so I will have to get three prices."	"The cheapest will get the job, no matter what the quality, service, skill, delivery, etc., might look like."	"Does that mean that the cheapest will get the job, no matter what the quality, service, skill, delivery, etc., might look like?"
"I was really hoping for more of a discount from you at this stage. Can you come down any more?"	"I receive a bonus based on the savings that I can deliver."	"I could go back to my boss for a discussion on this for you. I'm not saying that we can do anything on the price, but let's pretend we could. What more can I tell my boss that we would get from you in terms of length of contract or increased commitment if we could?"
"Can you give the buying team a proposal demonstrating how your firm might deal with a few particular challenges?"	"I don't want to pay an external company to do any research for us. Can you come train us all for free with no commitment whatsoever from us to do anything for you afterwards?"	"Well, thanks for the vote of confidence, but before I mobilize our team, let's agree first what would happen if your team genuinely liked what they saw from us. Is that fair?"

Prospect Translation Guide		
When prospects say…	**…they might actually be saying…**	**To verify, ask something like…**
"If we give you the order today, can we jump the queue, and can you guarantee us a short lead time?"	"Your competitor has let us down at the last minute—or we screwed up and didn't order the stuff early enough—or we didn't have the money/cash/funds to buy earlier, and now we're in the quicksand. Help!"	"I don't know; possibly not, at this late stage. I'll certainly see what I can do to help. What will the effect on your business be if we say 'yes,' or, more importantly, if we say 'no'?"
"You would need to significantly improve our buying terms for us to even consider you. Your competitors give us an extra 60 days to pay."	"We are strapped for cash, and we are only coming to you now to spread our credit."	"I'm not sure I understand what you're saying to me. Are you saying that if we can improve your terms to get closer to our competitors', you would definitely give us this particular order along with every single order from now on?"
"I will get the purchase order to you next week."	"I can't think of what else to say to get you out of the office, but as soon as you go, I will send an email cancelling the order."	"OK, great. Can I tell you my biggest fear, though? I'm worried that I possibly pressured you into this decision, and maybe it's not really what you wanted to do. Am I right?"

Prospect Translation Guide

When prospects say...	...they might actually be saying...	To verify, ask something like...
"Can you give us a PC sum for the following scheme, and have it back to us by next week?"	"Do some work for me, for free. Nothing will happen, but I'm doing a broad feasibility study, and I need to find a firm dumb enough to send me a working scheme for free—but, hey, that's just the way the world works, right?"	"Well, thanks for asking. Of course, I can, but before I get started, why? What's going on? Why do you need it so quickly? And, why us? What's behind the request, and, more importantly, what will you do with the quote when you get it?"
"I'm the decision maker."	"I'm not actually the decision maker, but I didn't get enough recognition and love from my family as I grew up. I now use my position to beat up people like you—it makes me feel better about myself."	"Glad to know it. Of course, when decisions like this get made for this kind of contract at this kind of money, there's almost always a few others involved too. Once you've given it the green light, who else typically sees it for final rubber-stamping?"

Prospect Translation Guide		
When prospects say…	**…they might actually be saying…**	**To verify, ask something like…**
"We're looking for a new supplier, and we've heard good things about your company."	"Our old supplier has let us down once too often, and we are tired of them messing with us." …or… "We're happy with our current supplier, but we want to use your quotation to beat them up on price."	"Lovely. Our reputation is important to us. What have you heard, and from whom, and what's gone so badly with your current supplier that you're even talking to us after working with them all of these years?"

Make sure that you and the prospect (and customer) are all on the same page. If you take what the other person says at face value, you're almost certainly in separate mindsets. Questions like the ones you just read get everyone on the same page, sharing the same intent—so keep plugging away, slugger. That's how you qualify prospects.

Smart questions like the ones in the table above help you separate the wheat from the chaff. They start to qualify the depth of interest that your prospect might have in developing an ongoing relationship with you. They elevate your attractiveness and the value of your position in the perception of the prospect. Let's face it. You have some valuable experience, knowledge, skill, products, and services, and they're not easily won. People should have to work hard to get your stuff. You're not for everyone, after all.

When prospects realize that you value your own time (and effort, self-interest, resources, and energy) as much as they value theirs, things will start to change for you for the better. You'll have lots more time to find and pursue genuine prospects. Although your manager might see your busywork output drop, your revenues will climb. Better qualifying through better questioning is what gets you to this better place. By asking more and better questions that help you disqualify your prospects in a better way, your sales effectiveness and efficiency will dramatically rise.

It's a lot like dating. The person who plays hardest to get often ends up being the most desired one of all.

CHAPTER SUMMARY

- Qualify hard, close easy.
- Don't become addicted to "hopium." Keep asking questions to make sure what you think prospects said was actually what they meant and not simply what you hoped to hear.

> *"I know that you believe you understand what you think I said, but I'm not sure you realize that what you heard is not what I meant."*
> —Robert McCloskey

CHAPTER 13

The Universal Yes

Whenever you think it's time to tell the customer something, it's typically not.

Instead, it's time to frame what you want to get across in the form of a question. And you know what? Some questions are all but guaranteed to elicit permission for you to move one step closer to the goal line.

Imagine that you're in front of a customer/prospect, and you desperately feel that you have something that simply needs saying. You feel a terrible burning compulsion to advise the prospect why your stuff is so much better than your competitor's stuff. You've read all the brochures and tech-specs, after all, and you're simply bursting with clever things to say and new clever data to impart. You've got a degree in this stuff, for crying out loud (and the commensurate student loan with 35 years still to pay off), so that prospect better well just quiet down, sit there, and listen to how clever you are, how experienced you are, and how much good stuff you know. Right?

As soon as prospects hear what you have to say, they're bound to buy. I mean it makes perfect sense for them to buy if you just bury them in enough compelling, logical sales stuff. Feature, function, benefit—everyone knows the mantra, right?*

Undeterred, and simply brimming with all of the clever stuff that the marketing and new product development people told you at the sales convention last week, imagine that you say to the prospect:

> "Prospect Person, here's why our Super-Gizmo gadgets are so much better than Super-Gadgets' gizmos."

...or...

> "Prospect Person, here's why we feel that it's so important these days to consider taking our fully-inclusive, no-quibble, 24-hour customer service hotline Gold Package, VIP support scheme."

...or...

> "Prospect Person, my manager specifically wants me to mention this next thing to you before it's too late."

> (Without actually mentioning, of course, that you make really good margins on the sale, and most of your commission check is based on sales by the end of the quarter, and your spouse really wants that new designer luggage, and you'd feel like such a heel if you can't get it since you've been on

---

* You were not supposed to agree with any of that, by the way. Just pointing that out.

the road for three months and have hardly even seen your kids in ages...)

Anything that sounds in any way like any of the above is, let's agree, very bad. Why? Because it sounds like sales speak, which inevitably translates as, "I bring this up now because it is good for me and maybe bad for you, but who cares?"

Sure, comments like this get your needs met—your parent's voice booming in one ear with what a clever person you are, and your sales manager's voice in the other ear urging you not to forget to tell the client what the marketing people said about the new material being 0.3% lighter than the nearest comparable product from overseas, etc., etc., ad nauseam.

Truth is, buyers can all feel when someone is making a move on them and when they are being sold to, and they simply don't like it. Their shields go up, they set their phasers to stun, and they make plans for a quick escape. Remember, telling is not selling—not effectively, anyway. Even if it were,* people don't want to be told or sold.

Wouldn't it be much better if you could position things such that the prospect actually wants the salesperson to keep talking? If there were a method that you could utilize to get your point across in such a way that the prospect doesn't feel the specter of the sales move? That surely has to be better. So, how? Well, guess what? It's by asking the right sort of questions again, that's how.**

Let's imagine that the prospect asks for a quotation based on half a container of whatever you are selling these days.

You might be tempted to say:

---

*   Which it's not.

** Are you picking up on the pattern yet?

"Let me tell you why it maybe makes sense to order the full container so close to the month end..."

Guess what happens if you do, though? The prospect immediately resists. He figures out in a nano-second that you're only after the commission check, that you're close to your sales targets, that he will end up with half a container of crap that he can't move on, and that you're only suggesting the increase in order size for reasons that are extremely good for you and that are maybe bad for him.

This is not the way to go.

Why not ask instead:

"Shall I tell you my biggest fear about you ordering only half a container at this time?"

If you ask this unusual and slightly unexpected question (in a very "struggling" way—with a big sigh, cow-eyes, looking slightly crestfallen and wounded), the prospect doesn't feel that he's being sold.

He will probably say something like, "Sure, of course, go ahead." His interest will have been piqued, and he will be a little more receptive. His phasers will not be on stun.* With this new type of play, he stays emotional, not intellectual—more on this later.

Once you ask a question like that, if you then get permission to tell your side of the story—ideally with a third-party story thrown in—then great. (More on third-party stories later.) Permission from the prospect to keep talking is, as far as the prospect is concerned, not selling. You're just doing what he asked you to do, which is telling him more.

What if you were skillful enough to ask questions in such a way as to almost always get a positive response or permission to continue?

---

* In fact he may even be calling sick bay to have a nurse and a comfy bed on standby for you.

Wouldn't your selling life be enhanced if you were a proponent of this kind of permission-based selling—the art of asking, not telling or selling? Helping prospects discover for themselves that they have a need for your stuff is right in line with Sandler Rule #15: "The best sales presentation you'll ever give, the prospect will never see." For more on Sandler Rules, see the aptly titled book, *The Sandler Rules*.

ANOTHER EXAMPLE

Imagine that you're Tamara, the buyer.

Imagine that you're talking to the representative of XYZ Company.

Imagine that you ask the salesperson Raoul this question: "Raoul, tell me why you think that I should pay 5% more from you at XYZ Company than from my old pal at ABC Company whom I have been using for almost three years now?"

That's a genuinely tricky question. It's not easy to answer in a way that doesn't make it sound like a big pile of natural fertilizer.

OK. Take a second to think how you would answer this question, knowing what you know right now.

Try thinking of a worthwhile/valuable and gentle response— one that doesn't sound defensive, evasive, or "sales-y," and one that allows both the buyer and the seller to be on grounds of equal business stature.

Drawing a blank? OK. What if you were to say something like this?

"That's a great question, Tamara [stroke]. Why should you consider using us instead of ABC Company, when we're about 5% more expensive than they are [repeat/restate/rephrase]? Well, maybe you shouldn't, Tamara. But shall I tell you what most of our other customers tell us?"

Nice. Not pushy. Not desperate. Not defensive. What is Tamara possibly going to say to that? She's going to say "yes," right? Right!

Not a bad opening proposition, eh? Phasers not on stun, interest piqued, right? An emotional, not an intellectual response from Tamara—good.

Or how about this, as an even better gambit.

"Tamara, that's such a smart question [stroke]. After all, 5% is probably a lot of money, right [repeat]? Well [struggle—sigh—look worried—fidget in your chair], can I tell you what my biggest fear is right now, Tamara?"

Again, what is Tamara going to say to this—"No"? Of course she's not. Any buyer hearing that will say something like, "Go ahead. What's bothering you? What's on your mind?" She stays in an emotional, not a reptilian mindset—great.

Or, how about this?

"Tamara, I'm so glad that you asked me that [stroke]. What can we possibly add that is maybe worth 5% more than the other guys [repeat]? Well, I was thinking about this meeting last night on the way home. Can I take two minutes to tell you what I was thinking?"

Tamara will be on the edge of her seat, smiling like Alice's Cheshire cat, and hanging on your every word. You sound nothing like the last salesperson she spoke to. "Really?" she's thinking. "You were thinking about this last night? What's that all about, I wonder? Tell me more..."

Whatever you now say to Tamara has been invited by her. She has asked you a question, and she feels intrigued about what you're going to say next in an emotional way, not an intellectual way.

Remember, David Sandler pointed out that people make decisions emotionally and justify them intellectually. The more you can keep your discussions with prospects emotional, the better for you by far. Don't ever simply answer why you're 5% more expensive, answer why you deliver 5% more value—and frame that value in emotional, not intellectual terms.

Let's continue with our scenario.

Remember, Tamara has asked why you're 5% more expensive than the other company. Instead of going into defense mode, you say something along the lines of, "Tamara, that's a great question. It's one that I get asked a lot, of course. Can I tell you what's been bothering me?"

What will Tamara say? You already know that. She will say, "Of course, go ahead."

That's when you say something like this:

"The reason that I've been getting a little heartburn in talking to you this morning is that we always know that we're about 5–10% more expensive than the other team. I always worry that my new prospects won't give me the chance to explain to them what our other great customers tell us after they have used us for the first time. I'm so glad that you've brought that up and given me the chance to explain. Would it make sense to take, oh, I don't know [huff, puff, struggle a bit], two minutes to explain what's typically going on in situations like this?"

What will Tamara say to this? Again, you already know the answer. She will always say, "Of course, go ahead."

Or, how about this?

"The reason that I've been worried, Tamara, is that we always know that we are always about 5–10% more expensive than the other team. I hate this question coming up so early in the conversation, but why do you think that maybe we are always there on price, toward the upper end of the other quotes that you can get elsewhere or on the internet?"

How will Tamara likely respond to this response?

If it's anything like, "Well, maybe it's because of your service?," then you ask, "Partly, yes. Shall I tell you a little more about what our customers say about our service packages?"

If she says anything like, "Well, I don't know, is it something to do with your manufacturing quality?," then you say, "That's it, Tamara! Do you want to know what our other customers tell us are the top three things about our manufacturing quality levels?"

If she says anything like, "Your after-care support, maybe?," then you ask, "After care, of course, nice one, Tamara. Do you want to know what we hear most about our after-care programs?"

You get the idea.

- Tell prospects that you've been worried/afraid.
- Ask them if they want to know what's been bothering you—they will always say "yes."
- Explain why things are the way that they are with you and your company/quotation/structure/geography/price/service/payment method/materials/partnerships, etc., etc., and what other great customers, customers like them, tell you about why they are so happy with the issue that you're discussing.

Remember, prospects are asking you for the information, so you're now not selling to them. You're not pitching to them; you're advising them—super, big, hairy difference.

These kinds of fear questions can put an entirely different complexion on your selling process. Consider where you might be able to insert them into your daily repertoire and the positive effect that they will have on your conversations and conversion rates.

Here are some more questions to ruminate over that might get Pete Prospect saying what you want him to say, namely: "Sure, tell me more."

"Pete, can I tell you what I've been worried about?"

"Pete, shall I take a second to tell you what others in your sector tell us?"

"Pete, would you like to know what research says is the number one buying decision criteria from buyers in your industry today?"

"Pete, would it make sense to tell you what we found when we spoke to other buyers just like you on this subject?"

"Pete, that's a good question, let me answer that by asking you a quick question first. Is that fair?"

"Pete, rather than directly answer that, let me first ask you this. Would that be OK?"

"Pete, it might make sense to tell you what a customer of mine told me last week when he first noticed that. Would you mind?"

"Pete, can I come straight back to that question in a second, and first ask you why that question specifically is your most important one?"

"Pete, can I just take a second to check that I'm properly understanding what you're asking me? Would that be OK?"

"Pete, I was hoping that you'd ask me that. Do you want to know why?"

"Pete, that's such a great question. Can I explain what's so smart about it?"

To any of these questions, Pete has very little option other than give you permission to continue. These are what I call "universal *yes*" questions.

When you ask that kind of question, the dynamics shift a little in your favor. At that moment, the information that comes from you next is not selling—it's advice. As far as Pete is concerned, advice is a good thing. We already know he thinks selling to him is a bad thing.

You will know that you have the question just about right when Pete gives you his full interest and permission to go ahead. The question that elicits a universal *yes* is the right question because it transforms you from a dime-a-dozen salesperson into a trusted advisor.

THE UNIVERSAL YES IN ACTION

Assume you say to a prospect, "Can I take five minutes to tell you why our company is so great, why you should consider using us, why we are better than all of our competitors, and why you'd be crazy not to buy from me today?" Ugh! What does the prospect feel when hearing that? He feels that you're selling to him. Repeat after me: That's bad. That's a very bad thing.

Now assume that instead you ask, "Our new customers typically tell us two things: 1) that they're perfectly OK paying a few more percentage points with us over the price of our competitors; and 2) they understand why we have to build up stock for them over time. Before we even get started, would it make sense to maybe take a minute to explain why they tend to tell us these things and why they seem to think that way?"

Can the prospect genuinely say, "No, thanks"? Those are the exact things that he's worried about, too. Prospects will say "yes" to that kind of question—it's a universal *yes*.

SOME MORE HOMEWORK

So, how about this for an extension to your last homework assignment? How about you now invest in a pack of 3"x5" postcards? How about you write on each card in big black letters those same 20 very typical (but tricky) questions that you get asked in your everyday sales world? Then, take the time to figure out a question that you can ask in reply, which elicits a universal *yes* from the prospect/customer. Then, write and practice the questions to use after that.

AN ADVANCED TECHNIQUE

So, how about this for an even stronger/deeper wrinkle: Instead of waiting to be asked why you are 5% more expensive than the last guy, or why you need two weeks longer lead time, or why you require 50% deposit on an order, or why you do full credit checks, etc., why not be the first to mention the touchy issue, whatever it might be?

Wow.

Talk about not looking or sounding like a salesperson, right? Yes, it takes some real guts—about five-seconds' worth—to really alter the whole tenor of the dialogue in a new sales encounter. As David Sandler says in one of his timeless 49 Sandler Rules, if there's a bomb to go off, why not explode it yourself first? (See Rule #23.)

Why not do this?

> Meet with the new prospect; shake hands, and talk about the weather and the price of fish (but only for a couple of moments, tops). Then say something like, "Well, down to business, I guess, Pete. Hey listen, before we even start looking at the plans for your new annex [or whatever it is that you do for a living], can I tell you what I was thinking about this morning when I was going over today's meeting in my head?"

It's a universal *yes*, I promise. You continue:

> "Thanks. So, look, we work with really great architects and designers, just like you, who often ask us two things when

we meet face-to-face for the very first time: 1) how is it that we are slightly more expensive than most of our competitors; and 2) why do we always insist on a 5% deposit? Would it make sense, Pete, to take a few minutes before we even begin, to maybe just explore those two issues? What do you think? Does that sound fair?"

And you score yet another universal *yes*.

FIVE REASONS WHY THIS IS A GREAT OPENING SALES STRATEGY

1. The big issue(s) are out on the table and get discussed very early on. Remember, if these issues are going to blow up the relationship and it's going to be a *no* because of them, when do you want you know? That's right—right away.
2. Once the prospect has accepted your limitations, he can't beat you up with these issues later on—usually by demanding a price concession to which you invariably cave because you've already invested so much time getting to that point and your spouse has already spent the commission check on a new pair of skis.
3. You immediately relax. Your shoulders go down and you can breathe easy because you're not perpetually dodging the tricky issue that you just know will surface at some point anyway. Even if he doesn't figure it out, your competitors are sure to mention it to him when they discover that you're getting the order.
4. The cover comes off the elephant in the room—and you can have an adult conversation about it before anyone is too invested.

5. You don't sound/feel/think/look like any other salesperson he talks to—which means, equal business stature. Excellent!

So, now let's go back to those 3"x5" cards you will be putting together. Instead of waiting for the top two tricky questions to come up (questions I know you will have great response questions to), why not start your next sales interview with those very issues? You bring them up first. Get permission to get them out on the table early on, deal with them, and move to the next step—or not. But at least your efficiency and effectiveness ratios will go through the roof.

Now you're starting to operate at the higher levels of skill and competence.

Nice.

CHAPTER SUMMARY

- By asking questions that elicit the universal *yes*, the sales process stays on track and you control the flow and speed of information, not the buyer.
- Keep the momentum high—learn to ask killer questions.

> *"If you do not ask the right questions, you do not get the right answers. A question asked in the right way often points to its own answer."*
> —Edward Hodnett

CHAPTER 14

Good Questions Lead to Good Answers

Asking good questions inevitably leads to getting good answers. The converse, of course, is also true: bad questions lead to bad (or at any rate, unhelpful) answers.

For instance, consider a question like, "How's your week going?"

Lazy. Pointless. Cliché. If you think this is a bonding and rapport question, think again. This question actually reduces your status in the buyer's world because even though it's meaningless, the person feels compelled to answer it out of a sense of common courtesy. How accurate does the answer have to actually be? What can you possibly learn? Most time you'll hear non-specific platitudes, "Oh, not so bad, up and down, you know. Could always be better. We soldier on."

So now you know. A dumb question leads to a polite (and pointless) answer. Here are some more dumb questions:

- "How are you today?"
- "How's business?"
- "Who are your top competitors?"
- "Who are you trying to target?"
- "Is that your sailfish in the photo on the wall?"
- "Are those the grandchildren? They're adorable."
- "Aren't we having a lot of mild [or intense, or otherwise adjectival] weather for this time of year?"

These are all lazy, trite, tired, and downright dumb questions.

Most lazy questions make you sound like the cliché sales amateur. By this point, you know who I mean. The kind of salesperson who asks:

- "Would you prefer it in red or blue?"
- "I'm in your area next week. Which day might be best to stop in to say 'hi' and show you our latest catalogue?"
- "What keeps you up at night?"

Such cliché questions are just as unimaginative, lightweight, and unforgiveable. Avoid them!

Without wanting to sound too cliché, you should avoid cliché questions like, well, the plague.

It's easier than you might imagine to fall into the trap of asking questions that are that stupid. Often, it's a reaction to stress. If you have the ability to record yourself in a few sales interview role-plays (and yes, those count as stressful situations), please do so. Then listen to the recordings. I predict you'll be amazed and horrified to learn just how often you fall back on asking trite, unimaginative, dead-end questions.

Lazy, ill-considered, tactical, and superficial questions can end up presaging trouble for you and your cause. They almost always waste time, cause friction, and lengthen the sales cycle—exactly the opposite of what we at Sandler are trying to teach you to master.

Once you have recorded yourself in a few sales interviews and have gotten over the horror and shock, take time to devise better questions—questions that have real purpose and serve to propel you to your ultimate aim, that of reaching a clear decision. (Often, that decision is "No!," which, as we have already seen, is perfectly OK. If it is going to be a *no*, when would you like to know? ASAP.)

Our goal here is to eliminate the same-ol,' same-ol' questions that all of the same-ol,' same-ol' sales dogs ask. Remember, for prospects to see you as better, first they must see you as different. You can't be better and the same.

Asking better questions is what makes you better.

SHORTENING THE SALES CYCLE WITH KILLER QUESTIONS

In broad terms, whatever you can do to shorten the sales cycle (or speed up the ultimate *yes/no* decision) is good. Good questions propel you forward; bad questions do not.

As an exercise in asking smarter questions that propel you in this way, consider the elements/stages of the Sandler Selling System explained at the beginning of this book. As you recall, we examined how David Sandler codified his new sales process into a submarine model. In each segment of the process, there are dozens of little truths to uncover before moving on to the next step in the process.

Sometimes we see that salespeople get so embedded and encamped in a particular issue that it's almost impossible for them to find a way to get out and move to the next level. In effect, they refuse to move forward to the next compartment of the submarine, possibly because the next stage intimidates or worries them. For example, they may be a little reticent to talk about money (the client's budget) so they avoid that step.

Fortunately, there are questions that help you transition easily from one step of the sales process to the next—called, predictably and perhaps boringly, transitioning questions. Sometimes we call these, the "killer questions" because they are wonderful at propelling the prospect (and yourself) through the pipeline toward an answer—a decision.

Take time to think about and modify these questions to fit into your situation. You may want to type them into your computer and print them on a sales crib sheet. Learn when to use them. Practice them. They will keep the pace and the emotion on the sales call high as you get permission from the prospect to keep moving from one section of the submarine to the next.

Notice that most of the questions below elicit a universal *yes*. If you can keep prospects nodding their heads and giving you permission to continue through your sales process while they feel in control, who is really in control of what's going on? Right—you.*

TRANSITIONING FROM BONDING & RAPPORT TO THE UP-FRONT CONTRACT

After talking (for a couple of minutes only) about the research that you did on your prospects' company (from their website or a Google search, for example) or the individual with whom you are meeting (from their LinkedIn page, for example), ask:

---

* Well done. Have a cookie, go on, you deserve it. No, not that one, the big one. Nice.

"Emily, shall we get down to business? Would it make sense to take a second to review last Wednesday's conversation when we agreed to put this meeting in our calendars?"

...or...

"Now then, Alice, let's just take a moment, shall we, to make sure that we're both still on the same page. Is that fair?"

...or...

"Alex, I'm just going to take a moment to go to the notes that I took when we spoke last week, just to make sure we get to cover everything that we agreed on. Are you comfortable with that?"

Each of these questions, and the ones that follow, are examples of the universal *yes*. Pepper your sales presentations with exactly these types of questions, and the effectiveness of your sales process will dramatically improve. So, too, will the speed of prospect qualification/disqualification, as well as your sales conversion rates. These are critical question types to master.

TRANSITIONING FROM UP-FRONT CONTRACT TO THE PAIN STEP

Once your prospect/client has agreed to the essence of the up-front contract that was made when the meeting was first established and you have clarified that nothing has changed that might influence or affect the meeting, you are now ready to transition to the Pain Step.

"So, Julie, we talked briefly about having a look at your new website. Shall we start by maybe outlining the top three or four things that you were hoping to see from me today?"

...or...

"Carlos, most of our clients tell us at this early stage that they're not quite sure how we do what we do. Would it make sense for me to take a moment to describe how our process works and what kinds of things we typically do? Then maybe you can take a second to tell me little bit about what that might look like in your particular world or situation. Is that fair?"

...or...

"Grace, for me to try to figure out whether or not we might be a good fit, will you take a few moments to describe the most important elements as you see them concerning what we discussed on the phone and which of them means the most to you right now?"

TRANSITIONING FROM THE PAIN STEP TO THE BUDGET STEP

By this part of the process, you will have a much clearer picture of what your prospects want to see/feel/hear in order to close the gap between where they are and where they want to be—the pain gap. It's time to explore the investment required to close that gap:

"So, Mark, that all sounds like a lot. Let me see if I can summarize what you've said so far and if we can start to try to figure out a ballpark investment that might be required to sort all this out. Does that feel OK at this stage?"

...or...

"Well, Cristina, you know we don't do this sort of stuff for free. So let's see whether we are both in the same sort of ballpark for getting this sorted out—are you OK with that?"

...or...

"Effie, now that I think I'm beginning to see what's been going on, it would probably be a good time to start to discuss what you were hoping to see in terms of investments in time, money, effort, energy, organization, change, and so on. Does that feel like a good idea?"

TRANSITIONING FROM THE BUDGET STEP TO THE DECISION STEP

OK, we are getting close to the point where you can make a decision whether your prospect is qualified or disqualified. Before you can make this final assessment, you need to figure out who is important from the client's side in terms of making the purchase decision. Approach this phase of the interview as follows.

"Alan, before we agree on how I might best show you what our solution might look like, there's just a couple of extra things I'd like to explore with you. I don't suppose there's anyone else other than yourself who might also be really interested in the successful outcome of this project?"

...or...

"So, Patricio, usually when our clients make this kind of decision, there's always someone else who needs to be involved in the process. Would you care to explain to me who that is in your world?"

...or...

"Rick, when we present our solution to your buying team, we really want to make sure that everyone from the very top to the lower levels gets their views aired. So, who in your world is looking to have a say in the successful outcome of this particular project?"

TRANSITIONING FROM THE DECISION STEP TO THE FULFILLMENT STEP

This is the part of the process where you both have a decision to make. If you can show the clients/prospects a solution to their issues (pains) that accords with the conditions and constraints of their world, will they be on board, willing, able, and committed? If not, you don't present anything! (Remember?)

> "Natalie, let me recap what we have discussed. Then you can tell me whether I've missed anything, and if not, let me then try to figure out how important all of this is right now and how it stacks up against all of the other projects that might be on your radar. Are you OK with that?"
>
> ...or...
>
> "Dora, so that I can start to figure out whether we might even be able to help you, may I start by asking you one really critical question? When would you like to start? If we can't meet your deadline, everything else is kind of academic, right?"
>
> ...or...
>
> "Maureen, let's pretend, just for a quick second, that we had the absolute perfect solution for you. I'm not saying we have, of course, but if we did, what would the next stage of the process look like in your world?"

TRANSITIONING FROM FULFILLMENT TO POST-SELL

If, after you have presented your solution to the prospect, you have to ask a question (or close) any tougher than, "So, Phil, what would you like to do next?," you've done something wrong.

By using the Sandler Selling System process, prospects will close themselves. If they don't, then the deal is already over and you have wasted you time. Ask for a referral; pack up; go home.

However, whether the lights are green (a *yes*), or red, you have to still remember the Post-Sell Step. You'll want to rehearse either the client or yourself on what to say/do next.

> "Paula, OK, glad that we have finally some clarity on the situation—thanks for sharing. Typically when we get to this stage it makes good sense to take a moment to have some clarity on the next steps from both sides; are you OK with that?"

...or...

> "Bernard, fine, I believe that you've made the right decision at this stage for your needs. Before I go, would you be comfortable taking a couple of minutes to make a clear record of what's next?"

...or...

> "Phillip, thanks for your candor. History tells us that if we spend a couple of minutes now documenting and agreeing on what's next, it saves a lot of confusion later—are you comfortable with that?"

KEEP MOVING FORWARD

Remember, your only job is to get to a decision—not to sell. To get to a decision, the process has to get to its conclusion—the ultimate Go/No-Go gate. You control the speed of every outcome by deciding when is the right time to move to the next step. You can figure out whether it makes sense to move forward to the next step by getting permission to do so with one of the universal *yes* questions I've shared here. Prospects feel relaxed, trusted, understood, engaged, and in control, too, because you ask their permission to continue every single step of the way.

CHAPTER SUMMARY

- Good questions are simple and keep the forward momentum high; bad questions are complicated and slow everything down—and often kill the whole thing.
- Universal *yes* answers give you permission to keep the conversation under control while giving the prospect/client the feeling of control—win-win.

> *"The quality of a question is not judged by its complexity, but by the complexity of thinking it provokes."*
> —Joseph O'Connor

CHAPTER 15

"How Much Time Will We Need?" —Questioning Master Class

In the prior chapter, we saw that asking smarter questions is a much stronger differentiation strategy than most salespeople dare to employ. How early in the relationship can you start employing this type of powerful questioning technique?

Earlier than you think.

Let's look at the very start of a sales conversation—as early as you can possibly get: the telephone cold call. It should end in a question that elicits permission to continue. Take a look.

"Hello, Barbara, this is Ted from ABC. I hope I haven't called you at a bad time. Would it be OK to take, oh, I don't know, maybe 30 seconds for me to tell you why I called, and then you can decide if it makes sense to continue? If it does, great; if not then I guess I'll get out of your hair forever. Does that sound fair?"

That's a nice up-front contract, set up with a question, which ends with a "is that fair" request/response.

Barbara will usually say one of five things which will sound something like the following:

1. **"Go ahead."** Great. Go for it.
2. **"Is this a cold call?"** Yes, it is, so say that it is. Barbara will either say "Go ahead," or "Go away"—either is fine.
3. **"No, thanks."** Great. Check that number off your list. Next!
4. **"How long will this take?"** Yes, you already said. So what? Say it again. Barbara will either say "Go ahead," or "Go away"—either is fine.
5. **"Can you call me back later?"** Great, agree to call back later—and ask what you should do if you can't get through at the agreed time.

Those are the five big responses.

Of course, Barbara could say, "You don't need to talk to me; you need to talk to Jack," or "I'm glad you called," or some other response for which you really don't need any help.

Whatever Barbara does say, there will be no need for an ambulance. No one will die. No blood will be spilled.

So relax—and make the call.

If Barbara says, "Yes" (or something like it), you simply get on with a description of the two or three main problems (pains) that your business solves for people just like Barbara (in 30 seconds or so).

Then, end with a question (what else?) that isn't too dissimilar from this: "Now I don't know much about what's going on in your world right now, Barbara, but did any of that make any sense at all?"

This approach/tactic generally elicits a binary *yes/no* response:

Barbara: No, not really.

Ted: OK, well, thanks for your time, Barbara. Say, before I get out of your life forever, two last questions, OK? One, are you comfortable enough for me to put you in our database so that we can reach out periodically to tell you what's new in our world?

Barbara: [Yes/No.]

Ted: OK; and, two, is there anyone else you care about who might benefit from us reaching out to them to introduce ourselves to them in the same way?

Barbara: Well, maybe.

Ted: Oh? Who?

If instead Barbara has said that Ted did make sense to her, the two will then have a brief discussion about the problem/pain about which he called. Then, depending on circumstances, Ted will need to suggest a move to the next step in the process. For the sake of brevity, let's assume that Ted is wanting a face-to-face meeting to discuss the issue. (*NOTE*: If, in your world, you want to send a quote or for Barbara to get out the credit card or to send you a form, etc., please modify this next bit of the dialog to best suit your particular situation—but remain as faithful as possible to the general thrust of the language, posture, positioning, and tone.)

Ted: Barbara, it sounds like it might make sense for you to invite me over to have a coffee and a talk about this. Is that fair?

Again, this is a fairly binary questioning strategy with little room for ambiguity or misinterpretation. It also allows you to flush out and measure the real depth of Barbara's intent/interest.

Barbara: Yes, but can you just email me some information for the moment? I'm very busy. I'll call you once I have reviewed your email.

This is most likely a *no, thanks*, dear reader. Any response like this should send you (figuratively) to Not OK-land. Confused. Unsure. Struggling. Your job now is to use this "struggling-ness" to figure out what's going on. Refer to the types of responses in the table in Chapter 12. If it's a *no*, when do you want to know? Find out the truth, then move on. Some will, some won't, so what, next!

What if she says instead:

Barbara: Sure, when are you thinking?

Yay! But don't get too excited at this point. This is not the time to overplay your hand. It is time now to get into ninja-questioning mode.

Ted: OK, let's see. Um, how about next Wednesday? Does that work for you?

Barbara: Sure. Three o'clock?

Let's not appear too keen.

Ted: Hmmm, Wednesday afternoon at three? What would happen, Barbara, if I said I can't make it Wednesday at three?

Yes. I want you to ask this even if you have nothing, zip, *nada, rien*, in your calendar on Wednesday at three o'clock. Did you really just read that? Oh, yes you did.

Posture, attitude, and guts, dear reader.

You haven't said you can't make it; you've simply suggested that you're a busy person, somewhat in demand, and that particular time might be a trifle inconvenient.

Barbara will likely say, "OK, then, Thursday at four," rather than simply killing it. In the unlikely event that killing does indeed happen, you will have to decide what to do next. One option is to appear to move things around such that Wednesday at three indeed becomes the appointed agreed slot.

Ted: OK, I've got you in for Thursday at four. Your place, I assume?

Now move to clarification.

Ted: Say, Barbara, how long are you putting in your calendar for the meeting?

Ask this! It's important.
Barbara will likely say either an hour (or other such appropriate timeslot that you can approve in principle) or ask how long you think that you'll need.

Ted: Well, I guess that it will only take ten minutes or so to figure out whether there's even a likely chance of a good fit or not between us. But history tells me that if we're still talking after 40 minutes or so, we are likely going to figure out how to do some business together. So, let's both put an hour in the calendar, and take it from there. Are you comfortable with that?

This is great posture and positioning. Relaxed. Conversational. Not desperate. Professional. Once she agrees, you move ahead.

Ted: I appreciate that, Barbara. Naturally I'm going to have lots of questions for you, like [insert three or four questions to illustrate what you would likely want to know—telegraph the questions to show that you're real]. And obviously you'll have lots of questions for me like [insert three or four questions that clients typically ask you when you first meet.*] Does that make sense?

Barbara will agree.

Ted: Super. Anything else to add to our agenda?

Count on it, nine times out of ten, Barbara will say "no."

Ted: Great. I have a couple of final questions for you then—is that OK?

Again, agreement.

Ted: Good. So, typically at the end of the meeting, Barbara, we will either agree to continue on to the next step (and frankly I don't know what that might even look like yet), or else we will agree to call it a day. Are you comfortable with that, too?

Barbara will likely agree.

Ted: Terrific. Um, I think that's about it for now, Barbara. Oh, who else do you think should be at the meeting with us?

Deal with the response to this. If Barbara says, "No one," great; if it's someone, be agreeable, of course, and also ask why it makes sense that that person will also be there.

Ted: One last thing. Whether the meeting goes well or badly next Wednesday (and both are OK, Barbara), my busi-

---

* Make sure that you have really good answers to these questions for when you are asked later. Don't suggest questions for which you don't have fantastic answers.

ness is built on a strong referral basis, so I may very well ask you for any introductions that you might have for me on the way out. Would that be OK, too?

Trust me. Barbara will say "yes." Even if prospects don't mean it, they will still say, "Yes," and you can remind them of that fact at a later stage, or not, as it suits you.

Tidy up, and finish off the call.

Ted will confirm the meeting by sending an email calendar invitation within the next 30 minutes or so. If Barbara rejects it, he's done or said something wrong; but if the tonality is right with the scripts and questions above, it won't be rejected.

Now we fast forward. When he get to Barbara's office on the allotted day and time and they've chatted for a few brief moments, Ted will ask something like this:

Ted: Barbara, when we set up this meeting last week, we said that we'd take up to [insert number] minutes to talk about [insert issue].

I said that I'd have to ask you lots of questions like [insert the three or four questions from the phone call], and you said you'd be wanting to ask me about [insert those three or four questions].

We also said that at the end of this meeting we would make a decision to continue or kill it, and that we would both be comfortable telling each other "no" if we felt it was the right thing to do, right?

And I think I said that I might even ask for a referral on the way out.

Are we both on the same page so far?

Anything other than a *yes* from Barbara at this point spells trouble—but if it has been set up right, there won't be any hostility.

Ted: Are we still OK for all of that, or has anything changed since we set this up?

Don't forget the, "Has anything changed?" question; it's really important to make this entirely habitual.

Ted: OK, so, Barbara, let's get down to business. Are you OK with that?

Just like that, you're off to the races.

MORE ADVANCED TECHNIQUES: FOLLOW THE FEDS

If you've ever been unfortunate enough to have been taken in for questioning by the smartly dressed ladies and gentlemen of the FBI, you will likely have been exposed to a variety of sophisticated interrogation strategies. (I have never been exposed to these strategies firsthand, of course, since I was nowhere near the docks at midnight on Thursday; I have never met Jimmy the Gent; and I have a watertight alibi anyway—I was giving out soup to the poor and needy of St. Cuthbert's. Just ask anyone.)

Poorly trained and inexperienced salespeople tend to believe that asking a few introductory questions and then talking a lot about their product's features and benefits, their company, and their clients is the best way to conduct the sales interview. They hope to build a picture of the prospect's situation over a period of time by piecing together all of the snippets of information that they glean. To a large extent, they never really check the facts nor question the validity of the prospect's story. I hope that by now, dear reader, you have figured out that this is not the way to get to the real truth.

The FBI distinguishes between two different situations requiring different questioning strategies: the interview and the interrogation. The FBI calls the interview, "a conversation with purpose." On the other hand, an interrogation is defined as "eliciting a confession against self-interest." Many salespeople approach a sales interview like they would an interrogation—and this is their first mistake.

Prospects feel like the sales meeting is designed to elicit some sort of confession against their own self-interest—i.e., them spending their money—therefore, they are guarded, suspicious, dubious, doubtful. This is not the kind of attitude that's going to help your cause. Decide, therefore, ahead of time, whether you are going to interview your prospects or interrogate them—there's a very big difference.

Two of the biggest mistakes that salespeople can make is to view the sales call as an interrogation, not an interview (mistake #1) or to let the prospect interrogate them (mistake #2).

Also, newsflash: FBI agents never go into an interview without some background information first. They research their suspect to the very best of their ability. They never just turn up and start firing questions (does that sound like any salespeople that you know?). Gathering as much background information as possible genuinely helps the agents shape the outcome of the interview. So, why do salespeople think that they are smart and experienced enough that they can just wing it? Let's agree that the days of winging it are over. Do your proper due-diligence beforehand.

Any successful FBI agent will also tell you that the truth is always hidden in small packages. The interrogation builds a picture of the truth as a jigsaw—little bits all fitting into one another to reveal the complete situation. The suspect (prospect) rarely blurts out all of the truth in one, long, all-revealing, soul-cleansing confession mere seconds before fading to the commercial break. This may happen on TV, but you're not on TV, are you?

It's up to the interviewer (salesperson), therefore, to start by putting the other person at ease—to build rapport. Tonality, as they train it at FBI headquarters, is the single most important method for achieving this. Anything that sounds in the least bit "interrogate-y" or accusatory is 100% bound to fail.

Prepare a set of questions in advance of the (sales) interview—not just in your head. Actually write them down. I don't care how long you've been selling or how many similar meetings you have been to. Do it. Why? According to the FBI, this is absolutely key to helping you "actively observe" every single word, nuance, syllable, sigh, and twitch when the other party is responding.

The truth, the Feds say, may well lie in the gap between milliseconds where you were thinking about the next question to ask rather than actively watching and listening to what is being said. Having a list of prepared questions is critical, even if you don't ask them all—see the back of the book for a good starting point or two.

Get the pace right, too. For most people, that means to slow down. Too many salespeople ask too many questions too quickly. Stop. Ask. Look. Listen.

The FBI trains agents to be as straightforward and matter of fact as possible in the interview situation (transparent and with some—but not a lot of—warmth and empathy). The trainers tell their recruits that in order to best control the interview, they should briefly introduce themselves and tell the interviewee where they work, what they do, and what they want. Refreshingly simple.

Other FBI tactics:

- Put the subject at ease. Ask a few questions about family, hobbies, the weather, etc.—but keep it short. Get the tonality in your voice right. Gentle. Nurturing. Keep rapport alive.
- Stay calm, and don't ever get emotionally attached to the case

or its outcome. Remain dispassionate. Keep checking "facts." Ask the same question in a few different ways over time. Assume nothing. Don't appear too keen to solve the case or accuse the subjects or their acquaintances.
- Tell third-party stories. Ask the subject to help you understand the story and the circumstances surrounding the events.
- Refrain from giving any unsolicited advice. Keep the status of the other person as high as possible.
- Ask a question, then allow suspects to completely finish answering. Never interrupt them. Resist finishing off their sentences, and always stay on subject. Acknowledge (don't dismiss) concerns. Don't belittle what an interviewee says, and don't ever assume anything.
- Close the interview by asking a few catch-all questions—these are often the most critical questions of all. Write all of these questions down. Learn them. Use them.
  ◊ "What else should I know about?"
  ◊ "What else should I be aware of?"
  ◊ "I feel that I've forgotten to ask something. Have I?"
  ◊ "Is there anything else you want to tell me?"

All of this should by now be starting to sound familiar—it's exactly how Sandler salespeople manage sales interviews, too.

ARE YOU INTERVIEWING OR INTERROGATING?

Your goal is to interview, not interrogate. Prospects like being interviewed. They don't like being interrogated.

Have a look at the two columns in the below chart. They should help you properly understand the main difference in philosophy and delivery between interrogation and interview questions. Whenever talking to prospects and clients, be sure that your ears are always on high-alert to spot which types of questions you're asking. Make sure that you get the tone of voice right, too. Be a Nurturing Parent or Adult who is in charge.

As a general rule of thumb, short questions are interrogation questions. They have their place too, of course, but not when you're trying to win a person over to sharing information more easily or readily.

Interrogation Question	Interview Question
"Are you the ultimate decision maker around here?"	"Typically when making this kind of decision involving this kind of investment in time and effort and energy, who other than you do you think it would be smart to also involve in the process?"
"Are you likely to simply choose the cheapest supplier option?"	"What do you expect to be the most important three things you will be considering when making a decision about choosing the best supplier for this new contract?"
"When will you make the purchase decision?"	"Can you help me to understand the process and timings involved in this project—from making the purchase decision to advising the successful supplier to expecting your final delivery?"
"Tell me a little bit about the history of the company."	"I've researched your company a little, of course, but I always find that the 'real' story is a little harder to find—although it's always much more interesting. What few things can you tell me about the business that someone like me wouldn't be able to find online?"
"So, why did you agree to see me today?"	"So, what are the few things that you were hoping that I might be able to help you with when we set up today's appointment?"

Interrogation Question	Interview Question
"How many people work in your company?" ...or... "What's your company revenue?" ...or... "Who runs the business?" ...or... "Who's your biggest competitor?" Etc.	"So that I can get a good feel for the business and not make any wild assumptions, which my partner tells me I'm very good at, can you give me a quick thumbnail of the business? Anything that you think would be useful for me to know, like how many people work at the company, what the board of directors' top priorities are, annual revenues, etc.—nothing that isn't in the public domain and might compromise you, of course."
"What have you tried to do in the past to fix this?"	"I'm guessing that this isn't the first time that you've thought about addressing this issue, but clearly there has been something that didn't pan out or meet your standards for resolving it. What things have you already tried that didn't quite work as well as you had hoped?"
"Why haven't you fixed this yet?"	"If you had a magic wand, what couple of things do you think might fix this issue once and for all? What things might stand in the way of you and those solutions at the moment, do you think?"
"How much money is there in the budget for this project?"	"Our clients normally tell us two things: 1) there's not much money in the budget for projects like this; and 2) they're not sure what the purchasing process might look like. How about we spend a few minutes trying to figure out which of these two issues might be the biggest challenge right about now?"

Mahatma Gandhi said, "In a gentle way, you can shake the world." Keep your tonality, your motives, and your approach gentle. You catch more flies with honey than with vinegar, remember. But you do need to mean it. It's very easy to spot fakes—people who are only out for their own good, their own self-serving ends. It's no good having honey on your lips if there's larceny in your heart, dear reader.

If you want to fully understand the prospect and you want the prospect to fully understand you, then learn to ask gentle but probing questions that encourage the prospect to share information and remove any ambiguity (or assumptions that you might have) and get to the heart of the real truth. That's where the next order lies.

CHAPTER SUMMARY

- Interview your clients and prospects; don't interrogate them. Don't let your prospects interrogate you either—selling is a two-way street.
- Up-front contracts, posited with the right questions and intentions, will save your whole selling career.

> *"Understanding is a two-way street."*
> *—Eleanor Roosevelt*

CHAPTER 16

The Anatomy of a Sales Call

As we have seen, to significantly improve your sales batting average, you need a rock-solid sales structure. But you also need a plan and a review mechanism (process control system) for each and every sales interview.

The best way to be a truly self-sufficient and consistently improving salesperson is to properly understand, plan, and practice the three elements of each and every sales call (interview):

1. The pre-call plan (pre-mortem)
2. The call itself (sales interview)
3. The post-call review (postmortem)

Which of the three is the most important single element, do you think?

Most of the salespeople I talk to say #2—the actual sales call itself. That's where all the real action supposedly happens. I would submit, though, that all are equally critical. They all need equal levels of attention and focus in order for your skills and conversion rates to dramatically improve, to say nothing of the huge self-esteem and self-confidence improvements that they quickly bring.

In today's million-miles-per-hour world, sales managers often overlook these three critical elements of their managerial responsibility. Most salespeople never build up the muscle memory of doing these things properly. As a result they are never really held accountable for producing evidence for all three elements of the call, and, as a consequence, they never recognize the immense power, control, and positive effects that these elements bring to the table. That's a real shame. More importantly, perhaps, the organization has spent time, money, effort, and energy to get the sales meeting set up in the first place. Why risk all of that great work and effort by not paying attention to the final push that could well move the ball from the one-yard line into the end zone?

If you go into any call without having first properly planned and practiced the call, you will be fighting (so to speak) with one hand tied behind your back. That's no way to win a fist-fight.

If you're a sales manager, start insisting on these things as soon as possible. Build them into your CRM, if you must. If you are a salesperson whose boss hasn't yet seen the light, start doing them for yourself. If you do, you'll likely be the sales manager yourself before too long.

Let's take a look at all three elements in detail.

PRE-CALL PLANNING

The objective that you should be working toward here is to proactively attempt to shape a positive outcome for the sales call. This is the part of the process that gets most ignored, however. Here are the three big reasons I hear to skip pre-call planning.

1. **Too basic.** You think you're experienced enough not to have to bother with such trifles and distractions. You're a product-knowledge expert, and you've done this a thousand times before, after all; you've been around the block enough times to know what's what. Clever old you.
2. **Too little time.** You're rushing at a million miles per hour from one call to the next. In today's economy, companies always try to get more output from fewer individuals, territories get ever bigger, and responsibilities grow; yet, it's still 45 miles and a 60-minute drive from Delaware to Dover. Who's got the time to plan? The pressure to hit your numbers is huge, and there never seems to be enough time in the day to give this part of the call proper focus and the attention it deserves. You'll drop a note or two on the next monthly sales report or a line or two in the new CRM system (that's what it's there for after all). Anyway, there's probably time to plan the next call in your head on the way to the next call. Clever old you.
3. **Too uncomfortable.** You're not really a systems-and-process kind of person. You're a true salesperson in every sense of the word—like those snappy talkers who can think on their feet, roll with the punches, and fast-talk their way out of any sticky situation. Charmers with the gift of the gab. Planning-shmanning. Clever old you.

If you think like any or all of the above, you're well and truly in your comfort zone—doing the same ol', same ol'—cranking the same ol' sales handle, getting the same ol' sales-sausages. If you're also in your earnings comfort zone, that's great; if not, you're going to need to change something. Guess what? You need to change this! If you want a different (better) output, you are going to have to change the input (how you sell).

As a rule of thumb, for a one-hour sales call, you need at least 30 minutes in prep-time.

Here is what you are going to spend that time thinking about:

- What is your up-front contract for the meeting? Your agenda, the client's agenda, the allotted time, expected outcome, and permission to ask questions. If there is no proper up-front contract in place, shame on you. Write one down now. Learn it. Start the meeting with it—it will be interesting to see what happens.
- Review what you have learned so far—what you know for sure, not what you think. Summarize what has happened up to this point, and what you know. What do you know about the prospects' pains, costs/budget, decision-making process, cast of characters, likely competitive reactions, etc.?
- What are your goals/objectives for the meeting? Have these be actually stated—and written down.
- What does a home run look like? What about a fallback objective? What does good look like?
- What do you believe (know) about your client's goals for the meeting? They are not always the same as yours.
- What things could the client likely ask you, and what will be your responses or reverses? Actually write the questions down. Take time now to think about the perfect response, not when you're 30 miles down the road after the call cursing yourself for not having been quick-witted enough for the killer comment. There are countless examples in this book.
- Figure out a great question to ask in response to all of these questions. This is a great way to look great. Don't squander these opportunities, dear reader—they don't come up that

often. This single skill alone, when well-developed and practiced, makes a real point of difference between you and all other salespeople your clients see.

- What minimum few things do you want to learn? Write down a set of at least 10 questions to ask (see the Epilogue for more help). Have two or three for each stage of the call—from opening things up to closing things off.
- Who's going to be in the room from the customer's side, and why? What do they each want to see/hear, and how will you manage the timing, speed, and dissemination of that information?
- If this is the first time that you have met any of them: How do you describe what you do? What does your 30-second commercial sound like?
- What will you say (or how will you respond) when under price, terms, or delivery-time pressures? Write down how you justify your value; then learn it by heart. Never try to justify your cost or your price, only your value.
- If you are with a colleague (or manager), which of you is going to lead the call? Hint: It should not be the sales manager unless the salesperson specifically asks for a life-line during the call. The sales manager's job here is to help plan/shape things before the call, to observe during the call, and to coach after the call.
- How will you manage the available resources for the meeting, including, critically, time management? Don't allow a two-call close to become a three- or four-call close.
- What's your selling style and list of questions for the call? This is dictated by where you are currently in the sales process.
- What does your ideal up-front contract look like for next steps following today, and how and when should you define it?

Rehearse what the call will look like ahead of time—just like an actor. Practice your scripts so that when the curtain goes up (or when the director yells out, "lights, camera, action"), you'll be instantly ready, relaxed, and rehearsed for your all-important close-up.

SALES CALL

The objective here is to qualify or disqualify the suspect, prospect, or client to either move along to the next step of your defined sales process or out of it.

This book has given you a wide array of things to consider, as well as things to say, and how to say them.

- Think about the Sandler selling process—where are you, and where are you headed?
- Ask lots of questions.
- Agree on very clear next steps—who does what next, why, and when?
- Agree on a new up-front contract. Lots of salespeople skip this because they're afraid of establishing an agenda for the next meeting will lead to a *no*.

Remember this key point: It's OK if the prospect tells you "No." If it's going to be a *no*, when do you want to know?

POST-CALL REVIEW

So, how did the call go? The objective that you should be working toward is to review the outcome of the call and consider how closely your objectives and the client's objectives were met. You also want to figure out who will be doing what next, of course—and what will happen if one or the other party fails to deliver on their side of the bargain.

To debrief yourself well, you need to develop a very keen self-awareness muscle. Only by being very concise, precise, and hugely self-critical (in a positive and non-damaging way) will you recognize what needs to be improved. Most salespeople operate alone, with little internal management, objective analysis, or observation. As such it is very easy to become lazy or self-satisfied. This is not how humans grow, improve, or develop.

A successful sales postmortem needs to be approached with you taking on the role of a true pathologist—dispassionately dissecting and analyzing every element of the call. There is a high need to be self-critical and self-aware. It's too easy to be self-servingly protective of your own self-image and to blame the prospect for everything that went wrong in the call. But the more you analyze and the better you get at it, the sooner you will start to see patterns. Is it every buyer in Wilmington, Delaware, who doesn't give you enough time to finish your story about the new research project that the business undertook? Or is the story (or maybe the way that you tell it) simply not interesting or relevant to your prospects after all? You grow by first recognizing the gap between where you are and where you should be, and post-call debriefing is one of the most powerful mechanism for this growth.

As close in time as possible after the call, take 15–20 minutes to formally consider what was done well—things that you need to do again, to embed, to make your successful behavior or belief habitual. Also do an analysis of things that need the most work in order to improve your sales effectiveness and efficiency. Prioritize action steps to improve these things.

1. Start your post-sell review by considering the outcome of the call. How close was it to the outcome for which you had hoped and planned? If there was a gap between the two, why?
2. Who is doing what next? We at Sandler call that the "clear future"—how close is the clear future to the plan that you had imagined before the call? Why?
3. Which questions did you answer well (by reversing) and which badly? Why?
4. How was your voice, your tonality? Did you speak softly, purposely, and slowly? Did you nurture? Did you leave your Child and Critical Parent voices in the car?
5. Which questions did you ask or position well? Why?
6. What did you say or agree to that you shouldn't have and why (showing off, most probably)?
7. What didn't you say that you should have and why (not enough backbone, most probably)?
8. As a consequence of the answers above, what will you start doing more of, stop doing altogether, or continue to do with even more determination?

Write these things down. Look at them every day.

How about this? How about we agree that from today you will commit to two things:

1. Define what the minimum elements of a post-call plan look like (something that can be done at speed, with minimum effort).
2. Define which few most-important calls will always be reviewed in such detail—especially #8 above.

These two things will change your life.

You're welcome.

A FINAL WORD

As a final word, isn't it amazing when two or more salespeople (or a salesperson and a sales manager) go to a sales call together, they always seem to find space in the calendar to meet ahead of time and sit down with a piece of paper to plan the call? Together, they decide: who will be asking questions, and who will be observing; who will be saying what, to whom, why, when, and how. There also always seems to be time to set aside to review the call together afterwards. Yet, strangely, when flying solo, salespeople always think that they can just wing it and hope for the best.

Think about that for a moment.

Find the time to get better at this stuff. It puts food in your stomach and shoes on your feet.

CHAPTER SUMMARY

- Don't forget the 8 P's: Proper planning, preparation, and practice prevents pathetic and poor performance.
- If you want to be treated like a professional, act like one.

> *"Tomorrow's victory is today's practice."*
> —Chris Bradford

EPILOGUE

Some of the Best Possible Questions to Ask

Remember, you're a business consultant and a trusted advisor, so behave like one. That means ask smart questions, then more questions, and then even more until you fully understand your prospects' situations and what they need in order to close the gap between where they are and where they want to be.

A vendor answers dumb questions; a trusted advisor asks smart ones.

The best way to get better at anything is practice, patience, and persistence. If you can, get a coach, too. You don't know what you don't know, right?

At Sandler, we teach:

Success = Failure + Persistence

Persistence has to become a habit, and practice has to be consciously targeted and applied.

Remember, you can't determine your future, but you can determine your habits. Your habits determine your future. Make a habit of asking more and better questions.

Whenever prospects or clients ask you a question, you need to figure out what's behind it. Then, when they ask it in a sales call, you can give a reassuring softening statement, repeat (restate or rephrase) the question, and ask what they mean or why they are asking that question at that particular time.

For times when it's your turn to start questioning (interviewing, not interrogating, remember), here is a short list designed to get your creative juices flowing. The list below does not follow any particular pattern, nor are the questions intended to be asked in any particular sequence.

Write down your favorite questions, and have them always at hand when you want to take charge of the interview, for when you hear crickets, or for when you see the tumbleweeds, well, tumbling.

Three things to remember: nurture, nurture, and then nurture some more. Be sure to get your tonality right.

For more questions like this—in fact, for a list of 125 of the very best questions to ask—visit: *sandler.com/asking-questions-tools*

For building rapport

- "Thanks for inviting me over today. Since we spoke on the phone, has anything changed?"
- "When we get to the end of the meeting, if we're both happy to move on to the next stage (and I have no idea what that might look like yet), let's agree to scope it out and set a date

in both of our calendars—that way we can make sure we stay on target. Is that fair?"

To start the ball rolling

- "Most of our time is spent helping businesses like yours. Tell me a little bit about how you go about dealing with _____ at the moment."
- "Would it make sense to start by telling me what's the single thing that gives you most concern about _____ right now?"

Near the beginning

- "If you were to imagine just two or three key things that you didn't like about your current solution or provider, what would they be?"
- "How would you rate things with _____ at the moment, from 1 (disaster) to 10 (perfect)?" Whatever the person says, you say, "OK, why?"

Understanding the pain

- "Have you ever considered giving up on solving this issue?"
- "If the situation didn't improve (or even got worse), how concerned do you imagine you or the business would be?"

To test understanding or to dig deeper

- "I don't suppose you could give me a good example?"
- "What do others in the department/company/office say about this issue?"

Near the middle of the conversation

- "I don't suppose you've given much thought to what performance standards you will be using to measure success on this issue?"

- "Let me take a moment to summarize what I think I've heard so far. You can tell me if I'm on the right page. Are you comfortable with that?"

When trying to understand the budget

- "Typically, when we get to this stage, our clients sometimes tell us that they have no money in the budget for this kind of stuff. Am I right in assuming that this is the situation here, too?"
- "Think of hotels. Are you imagining a 3-star, 4-star, or 5-star budget to get this fixed?" When the person answers, ask, "And that means what in terms of a range of price points?"

Understanding who else should be involved

- "In my house there are some decisions that are mine, and some that are 'ours.' How would you describe this one in your world?"
- "When a company such as yours usually buys this kind of stuff, for this kind of money, involving this sort of issue, or these many people, who has the final say?"

When you're trying to understand the timescales

- "What time frame are you working toward?" Whatever the person says next, ask, "Why so soon?"
- "What's most important: cost, quality, or speed?"

To get back on track when the sales interview is wandering

- "Can you tell me again about _____?"
- "Looking at the time we agreed to for this meeting, what should we discuss next?"

Near the end of the sale

- "Of all the things we have discussed so far, what am I missing? What have we left out?"
- "Why and under what circumstances would you consider giving us the opportunity to address these issues for you?"

To figure out if an existing account is at threat

- "Looking back over the last six months—off the record—what is the worst thing that we did that made you want to throw us out of here?"
- "Let's be straight with one another. You've given us business over the last year. Was it worth it? Where did we let you down?"

When teeing things up for a referral

- "I'm guessing that you don't know any other businesses like yours who are experiencing similar sorts of issues?"
- "Imagine that things go well, and you give us the order. What would be the best way for me to ask you for a referral at the end of all of this?"

For meetings involving groups

- "What's the one key issue that the group all believes needs addressing first?"
- "It's hard to present to a group. Who is really making this decision today? I'll try to keep taking that person's temperature most; is that fair?"

When presenting your products/solution/price

- "Before we continue, can we agree what the next step would be if you like what you see—and by 'like,' I mean you can see

we may have a solution that addresses all of the main points that we have discussed?"
- "Before I show you our _____ , let's take a few moments to recap everything that you said so far. Is that fair?"

If the buyer wants to think it over

- "That's totally understandable. Most of our customers need time to think it through. Could it be that you're worried about the cost, the implementation program, or not being too sure about what you've heard?"
- "Most of the time when I hear, 'Let me think about it,' what I'm really hearing is, 'No, thanks.' Tell me, is that what's happening here?"

When you feel the buyer is shopping your price/expertise

- "Are you looking for the cheapest price or the cheapest cost to get the problem fixed?"
- "If we can't get to within, say, 15% of your target price, what will you do next?" Whatever the person then says, ask, "What is your target price, and where did it come from?"

When the buyer gives you the order

- "What was the single best thing that swung it for us?"
- "What do you imagine your biggest three internal barriers to implementation might be?"

When you think it's a no

- "I get it, it's over; let's call off the dogs. Just before I go, where did I go wrong?"
- "Sounds to me that no matter what I said or what our solution could do for you, it still wouldn't make any difference—am I right?"

When making a cold call

- "Would it be OK to take 30 seconds to tell you why I called? Then you can decide whether it makes sense to continue. Are you comfortable with that promise?"
- "This is a cold call; shall I hang up first, or should you?"*

To ask a candidate who has applied for a job

- "Describe a job where you were challenged to learn many new things at once. How did you accomplish it, and what approach do you use to build new knowledge and skills?"
- "What has been the most difficult negotiation situation you've faced? What did you say or do to get it resolved?"

Some random good ones

- "What do you wish you had known about this issue six months ago?"
- "What does your family say you should do about all of this when you mention it to them over dinner?"

Questions for sales managers talking to their direct reports

- "What do you imagine will happen if you don't start finding new prospects to fill the sales pipeline?"
- "What are your specific plans to improve your sales conversion rates, reduce the sales cycle, keep key strategic clients, attain new in-profile clients, expand your client base, and regain lost clients?"

When writing your daily journal

- "What's my biggest single goal for the next 24 hours?"

---

* Make sure that you get your tonality right—lighthearted, please!

- "What one habit am I working on strengthening to help me best succeed?"

Strategic questions for senior executives
- "Let's pretend that these issues were somehow magically solved right now, today. From your perspective alone, how much better would the next one, three, and five years look?"
- "How critical is it to fix this thing? And how would you rate its importance?"

Bonus question since you made it all the way here

Ready? It's a good one. Here we go:

- "Good question; why do you ask?"

A final word: You should only ask a client, prospect, or a team member a question when you're not absolutely 100% sure what he feels, believes, or wants to know or understand.

Yet, how often can you be 100% sure of any of those things? Exactly.

For a comprehensive list of the Top 125 Questions (and much more of this type of business development dynamite), be sure to refer to Sandler Training at *sandler.com/asking-questions-tools*.

> "We are what we repeatedly do.
> Excellence is not an act, but a habit."
> —Aristotle

Look for these other books
on shop.sandler.com:

Prospect the Sandler Way

Transforming Leaders the Sandler Way

Selling Professional Services the Sandler Way

Accountability the Sandler Way

Selling Technology the Sandler Way

LinkedIn the Sandler Way

Bootstrap Selling the Sandler Way

Customer Service the Sandler Way

Selling to Homeowners the Sandler Way

Succeed the Sandler Way

The Contrarian Salesperson

The Sales Coach's Playbook

Lead When You Dance

Change the Sandler Way

Motivational Management the Sandler Way

Call Center Success the Sandler Way

Patient Care the Sandler Way

Winning from Failing

FREE DOWNLOAD
for readers of
ASKING QUESTIONS
THE SANDLER WAY

For a comprehensive list of over 100 specific Sandler questions you can ask during sales calls, visit:

sandler.com/asking-questions-tools

CRASH A CLASS AND EXPERIENCE THE
POWER OF SANDLER
YOU HAVE NOTHING TO LOSE AND EVERYTHING TO GAIN.

Are you a **salesperson** who...

- Feels uneasy about the lack of qualified prospects in your pipeline?
- Spends too much time developing proposals that do not turn into business?
- Wastes time with unqualified prospects?
- Continues to get 'think-it-overs' instead of closing?

Are you a **sales leader** who...

- Is frustrated with managing a sales force that's not meeting goals?
- Is tired of hiring salespeople that won't prospect?

Expand your reach and success by attending a complimentary training session at a local Sandler office near you.

REASONS TO
CRASH A CLASS

- Improve your current processes
- Go "beyond the book" and witness an interactive, in-person approach to a small group training
- Discover a workable, ground-level solution

Contact a Sandler trainer to reserve your seat today.
www.sandler.com/CRASH-A-CLASS